DISRUPT!
THINK EPIC. BE EPIC.

25 SUCCESSFUL HABITS
for an Extremely Disruptive World

BILL JENSEN

Disrupt! Think Epic. Be Epic. :
25 Successful Habits For an Extremely Disruptive World.

Copyright © 2013, William D. Jensen

Published by Net Minds Corporation under the Net Minds Select imprint.

Library of Congress Cataloging-in-Publication Data

Bill Jensen

Disrupt! Think Epic. Be Epic. : 25 Successful Habits For an Extremely Disruptive World / by Bill Jensen

    p. cm

    Includes index

    ISBN 978-0-9888795-2-2

1. Innovation. 2. Disruption 3. Organizational Effectiveness 4. Self-Help I. Title

HD58.95.J46   2013

658—dc20

Printed in the United States of America

USER'S MANUAL

Create your own disruptive handbook.

Do not read *Disrupt!* cover to cover.
It contains 25 successful habits for thriving in a disruptive world.
But nobody masters disruption all at once.

Pick five or six habits
that excite you,
scare you,
challenge you,
or have the most traction for
your current situation.

Go directly to those.
Ignore the rest of the book (for now).

Everything is in five- to ten-page,
bite-size chunks.
Ten minutes or less for each.

Bite off only what you need.
That's your personalized handbook.

CONTRIBUTORS

Author: Bill Jensen
my.netminds.com/BillJensen

Editor: Michael Martin
my.netminds.com/MichaelMartin

Copy Editor: Jenny Burman
my.netminds.com/JennyBurman

Interview Mind Mapping: Dan Boudin
my.netminds.com/DanBoudin

Indexing: Pilar Wyman
my.netminds.com/PilarWyman

Cover and Interior Design, Production: Mark Novelli, Imago
my.netminds.com/MarkNovelli

Marketing, Social Media: Cave Henricks Communications
my.netminds.com/CaveHenricks

Project Mentor: Tim Sanders
my.netminds.com/TimSanders

HOW THIS BOOK WAS MADE

This book was produced via Net Minds, a team-publishing platform that enables authors to find and join forces with talented editors, designers, marketers, and other publishing professionals.

We offer our authors the ability to grant each team member a stake in the book's long-term financial success, just like a startup.

Net Minds' authors enjoy the luxury of autonomy combined with skilled expertise.

To start a project or join a team, visit: NetMinds.com.

TABLE OF CONTENTS

SECTION 2

Don'ts [Things to Avoid]
4 HABITS FOR ENJOYING THE RIDE

SECTION 3
Guiding Principles [Live These]
7 HABITS FOR SAVING THE WORLD, HAVING A GREAT LIFE

Introduction
MASTER CLASS FOR THE REST OF US

Welcome to the age of continuous personal disruption.

Personal. Not just between titans of industry or *out there*. Continuous disruption is now a part of all of our lives.

Disruptions are anything that changes the course of your life or daily routine. They can be wonderfully good (a new baby, a technology that unleashes your creativity), or horribly bad (personal, family or global crises), or anywhere in between.

The Big So What

The people who will succeed in this era are those who figure out how to benefit from, or take advantage of, continuous disarray, disorder and disruption.

What's Different Now?

We used to be able to track major personal disruptions on a During-My-Lifetime scale. Which meant long settle-in times — those disruptions would eventually be easily manageable.

Quick example: the spark that changed the world.

You know it. Your life has been forever changed by it. It created complete disruption, everywhere. Billions of dollars were at stake. Upstart entrepreneurs were betting everything on competing technologies. And nobody knew which one would eventually go viral and change the world.

No, not the second decade of the 21st century.

The late 1870s, early 1880s.

Thomas Edison, as Steve Jobs would do 100 years later, combined other people's inventions and then worked tirelessly to perfect them in ways that no one had before. Results: the long-life incandescent lightbulb and the first system to distribute electricity to the masses. One of his employees, Nikola Tesla, would quit to launch his own startup because he felt his alternating current technology was better than Edison's. (AC vs. DC was the 1880s version of Mac vs. PC, iPhone vs. Droid.)

Within one month of building a power station in lower Manhattan, Edison Electric boasted 59 customers; a year later, 513. From that slow pace, it eventually went viral.

Your world was forever changed by this technological upheaval. Yet it hardly feels disruptive now. Worldwide, we just flip a switch or stick a plug into the wall. Easy peasy.

What's different today is that hundreds of personal disruptions are coming at you every day, and During-My-Lifetime or even "can you give me just a minute?"

settle-in times are quaint relics of the past. Excerpts from a typical day…

> "Senior team meeting in ten minutes. Some kid just launched a technology that destroyed 40 percent of our business."

> "That's the 27th Top Three Priority you hit me with this week!"

> Possible Headline: "Five-Person Malaysian Firm Reinvents Shopping"

Not so easy. For many, that means: Can't. Figure. It. Out.

That's why I wrote this book.

Disrupt! is for everyone trying to do extraordinary things while driving through a shitstorm of relentless disruptions.

The Goals of This Book Are To Help You …

- Learn the secrets of today's disruptive heroes
- Kick butt in a disruptive world
- Unleash what you already have

You already have much of what it takes to master successful habits in the age of personal disruption. It's time to free those qualities and skills.

About the 25 Habits

Disruption, by its nature, is a storm of ambiguity. Nothing is certain. Nothing is black or white. There is no perfect decision to be made.

And yet, we all have to figure it out … somehow.

I was reminded of this during a recent visit with my doctor. He spent more time grumbling about the massive disruptions in healthcare than he spent on me. "Tell us the rules, and we can play the game," he said. "None of us know what the rules are anymore."

That's what daily personal disruption feels like for many of us. Lawlessness. Chaos. No rules — at least none that are apparent.

Yet there are things you can do that will make that feeling disappear — think of them as the best practices for serenity and success in a disruptive world. The challenge: Most everyone who knows them is too busy disrupting things to walk us through them.

That's where this book and the 25 habits come in. I snagged 100 disruptive heroes and asked them for their secrets and advice. From them, I learned the most successful habits.

Master Class for the Rest of Us
Imagine asking 100 great disruptive heroes: How'd you do it?

Wow. It would be like sitting in on a master class on disruption with some of today's most successful pioneers! CEOs, inventors and scientists, entrepreneurs and freedom fighters, firefighters and doctors, geeks and a couple of freaks — heroes, all. Disruptive because they are challenging convention wisdom or simply do not accept the status quo. Great because they are helping us change for the better.

Among the 100 Heroes…

- Yahoo CEO — Marissa Mayer
- Hillary Clinton's head of innovation — Alec Ross
- World's best female poker player — Annie Duke
- Founder of StumbleUpon — Garrett Camp
- Founder of Flickr — Caterina Fake
- Film producer, *Avatar* and *Titanic* — Jon Landau

- Psychologist de-radicalizing boys   Feriha Peracha
  forced into the Taliban

(See back of the book for the complete list and selection criteria.)

About half of these heroes have been hailed by *Time, Fortune, Fast Company,* TED, PopTech, Davos, the Clinton Global Initiative and others as the disruptors who are taking us into the future.

Yet some of the most valuable and poignant insights come from unknown and unsung heroes: the Ugandan entrepreneur who built a sustainable charcoal fuel business; the IBM executive who is coaching the Chinese on LGBT diversity; the Goldman Sachs trader who left to launch the next Ticketmaster ... and dozens of entrepreneurs and executives just like them.

Although I collected their lessons learned and best practices, the greatest value may be finding yourself within their stories. In many ways, they are you — they hurt and love and have dreams like you, and they care and are dedicated like you.

Their story is your story.

When I say that you will learn the secrets of today's disruptive heroes, my hope is that you will find yourself within this book. If these heroes can summon the courage to do what they did, so can you.

The master class is actually a journey inward.

An Ongoing and Interactive Experience
As part of this book ...

- **Jump to YouTube**
  Highlights of every interview, all 100 heroes, are available online. You get to know them up close

and personal! (HD quality on all? Um, consider your expectations managed. Interviewees' connections, and thus video quality, varied.)

- **Bonus Materials**
  Check out *Click*, page 202, for how to access free online bonus materials like *Becoming a Triage Master* and *How to Blow Stuff Up and Get Away With It* and more.

- **The Courage Within Us:**
  Seven Essential Character Traits for Today's World
  I would never dream of cross-selling you (ahem), but … if you would like to learn more about disruptive character traits, a second book from these interviews is available — *The Courage Within Us*. I also asked the heroes "What makes you … you?" Their deeply personal insights are revealed in this second book.

Back to You …

Even if you don't see yourself as a disruptor — even if your role is to just keep things running — you still need to adapt to continuous disorder.

I ask everyone who reads this book to consider the following:

> Now that you know the habits for thriving in an age of personal disruption: How will you make of use them? How will you tweak them and make them your own?

No book does anything on its own. Changes in how you deal with or create disruptions can only be hard-won by you. I hope you see this book as your map for the amazing adventure that lies ahead. Enjoy the journey!

—Bill Jensen,
bill@simplerwork.com

SECTION 1
Dos

DO EPIC SH*T

14 HABITS FOR DOING GREAT WORK IN A DISRUPTIVE WORLD

"Life is an opportunity, benefit from it.
Life is beauty, admire it.
Life is a dream, realize it.
Life is a challenge, meet it.
Life is a duty, complete it.
Life is a game, play it.
Life is a promise, fulfill it.
Life is sorrow, overcome it.
Life is a song, sing it.
Life is a struggle, accept it.
Life is a tragedy, confront it.
Life is an adventure, dare it.
Life is luck, make it.
Life is too precious, do not destroy it.
Life is life, fight for it."

~ Mother Teresa

HABIT 1
QUESTION EVERYTHING

ASK THE QUESTIONS NO ONE ELSE IS ASKING

"How would you design a healthcare system if there was no such thing as doctors? How would you design it if intellectual property were invented differently — not so tied to chemical solutions?" asks this hero.

"The rules of the world in which we live are not written on tablets handed down by God. They are artifacts of our history. Most of them were done for good reasons, but sometimes those reasons have changed. And it's appropriate to reexamine the rules."

That's Jamie Heywood, co-founder and chairman of Patients-LikeMe, which is focused on reinventing healthcare.

His firm enables its members to bypass the usual double-blind, secretive approach to collecting and sharing health information, and opens it up so everyone can learn from everybody else. Members share their own data on their conditions, treatment history, symptoms, functional scores, moods and more. The result is a detailed longitudinal record that gives patients insights into their diseases that they could not obtain otherwise.

Heywood's quest began when his brother, Stephen, was diagnosed with ALS (Lou Gehrig's disease). The family searched the world for ideas that would help Stephen live a longer and better life and were not satisfied with what they found. Stephen died in 2006, but the family kept searching for better ways to fully understand one's own health.

Heywood typifies the first successful habit in a disruptive world — question everything.

"When I was doing discovery and clinical research with Stephen," he shares, "I thought of it this way: I don't work for the FDA and I don't really care what they think of what we're doing. Obviously, we're not going to break any laws. And the concerns they have are real issues that we want to address. But we'll address them with our own priorities and our own approach.

"I believe humanity is at a crossroads. We think we live in a free society because we're free to choose what computer we buy or where we live. But when you think about it, 17 percent of our GDP is in healthcare. What we need to talk about is the democratization of a system that completely fails from every transparency standpoint and from every cost standpoint. I want to invest in my parents being here for a long healthspan, but I have no way of making that investment because we have no holistic measures of health."

Heywood concludes, "One of my favorite personal values is 'challenge and respect.' You really need to respect what people believe and why they operate the way they do. But you have the right to challenge those assumptions."

Within Heywood's approach are two core ideas to remember for a disruptive world:

- Respect the people
- Question everything else

Many of our systems, structures, rules and approaches are holdovers from the Industrial Age and need to be completely rethought.

Everything Is Up For Grabs

We are in the midst of a massively disruptive era, where most every system or rule for how we do things has been, and will continue to be, up for grabs. From how governments deal with disasters to how businesses deliver value to how you care for own health, and much more — it's all being rethought and reinvented.

Whether you like that or not doesn't matter. It just is. Your parents' decision to have sex when they did puts you smack dab in the middle of the era of personal disruption.

The choice before you is simple. How do you want to face life? Reactively or proactively?

Extremely Proactive: The people who ask questions *that no one else is asking* are the inventors and entrepreneurs and leaders who will create the next wave of innovative disruptions.

Mainstream Proactive: The people who actively question most every system, structure, and rule placed before them and *then pick and chose which ones to ignore, work around or change* are the people who are taking charge of their lives.

Reactive: The people who *accept most everything as it's handed to them* will forever be holding on for dear life, waiting for the constant personal disruptions to subside.

Again: How do you want to face life?

Nothing Is Immune to Disruption

"No one is immune. Everyone is being touched," says this hero.

"The instinct is to feel that you are immune to these forces. But anything is now possible. One thing we all need to ask is 'What is currently analog that could be smarter, faster, stronger with data running through it, with a digital approach?' Leave the analog where it matters — where people need to connect with other people face-to-face — but pull it out where it doesn't."

That's Aaron Dignan, Founding Partner and CEO of Undercurrent, a digital strategy firm, which helps clients such as GE, PepsiCo and Ford stay ahead of their competition.

He continues, "Objects and information are starting to co-mingle in a very interesting way. Think about smarter everything. Think about: What is the information layer that's hiding within everything and how do we use that? Think about how little feedback we get every day from our bosses, our family, our friends, from our stuff. Did I do a good job today on my email inbox? I have no idea. And I think that's a travesty."

From our cars to our music selections to our training and development, everything is now being disrupted digitally. Every business is trying to get everything to run smarter, faster, stronger and cheaper. And the holy grail of the current age of disruption is getting all those digital things to talk to each other so everything you use and interact with is smarter — creating constant feedback loops and even better ways of doing things.

Those are the driving forces within a lot of the personal disruption coming at you every day, and which are causing so much rethinking of everything.

If You Want to Be Proactive, Begin Here...
Rethinking most anything begins with one of the following...

- What if... ?

  As in: What if the sun didn't revolve around the earth? (Galileo)

- Why... ?

  As in: Why does it have to be that way? (Steve Jobs, and most every child on the planet)

- Let's do it differently...

  As in: Let's ignore how it's *supposed to be.* (*Sgt. Pepper's Lonely Hearts Club Band*, Richard Branson)

But What Makes Those Work Is What's Inside Of You...
Your ability to question everything around you is directly tied to your ability to question your own assumptions and deeply held beliefs.

Which is why this habit is closely tied to several others:

- Know Thyself, Deeply (Habit 19)
- Follow Your Passion (Habit 20)
- Disrupt Yourself (Habit 22)

In a world of constant disruption, if you can't examine yourself on a regular basis and come to radically new conclusions about your role and what value you add and your strengths and weaknesses, it will be extremely difficult for you to examine all the status quo rules and structures that surround you.

You Gotta Have Street Cred

Think of the connection between the ability to continually question yourself and make adjustments accordingly as street cred for questioning other things.

"A big piece of who you are is your authenticity. If you've got something that you want get out there that's disruptive or runs against the grain, the first thing you have to do is build your own credibility for that," says hero Rusty Rueff who is an investor and advisor to multiple tech start-ups. Prior to that he was the EVP of Human Resources at Electronic Arts and was VP, International HR for PepsiCo.

"For others to trust you, to believe in you, they have to know that your motives are pure for the objective that you're putting out there," says Rueff. "There needs to be a consistency with who you are around a healthy dissatisfaction with the status quo. If you just show up one day after going with the flow and then start questioning things, that's so out of character."

A healthy dissatisfaction with the status quo begins with you — with your own status quo.

The Biggest Opportunities Lie in Looking At Things In Ways No One Else Is

Aluminum. Pretty ubiquitous and cheap, right?

From recyclable cans and the foil that covers your turkey to coatings that provide insulation to lighter automobile and jet plane parts — we have come to depend heavily on this soft, malleable metal.

But the only reason you have all that aluminum in your life is because somebody once asked the question no one else was asking: *How do we make it affordable?* In 1861, because it was so scarce and valuable, King Wilhelm of Prussia's crown was expertly crafted out of aluminum. We've gone from a precious metal reserved for royalty to wadding it up and throwing it at our kid sister after helping her with her science project made out of it.

That's an Industrial Age example. In today's digital world, the disruption opportunities are plentiful — available to anyone who's willing to question everything.

Aaron Dignan: "A lot of people are doing a lot of analysis, a lot of waiting and watching and asking: What are the best practices and who are the leaders? They're trying to measure themselves against what's going on in the present moment. There aren't a lot of people who are leaping ahead in a fearless way. The opportunities today require an ability to say 'I don't really care what anyone else thinks. I believe in my heart of hearts that I need to be moving forward and changing the way we do business.'"

What are the best practices? is the not the main question you need to be asking. That will just keep you in reactive mode, merely keeping up with the latest version of the status quo.

What today's disruptive world requires are everyday Galileos, who ask their own versions of: *What if our assumptions are wrong? How would that change how we think and what we do?*

What we need are ordinary thinkers and steel workers and farmers and nurses and managers, and, and, and ... Who believe we must do better if we are going to address today's wicked problems. And who tell us so. Who, with their probing questions, ask us to dream bigger. Much bigger.

Question Everything: Key Takeaways...

- Solutions to today's most wicked problems and biggest opportunities will come from asking the questions no one else is asking.

- You can only ask the questions worthy of pursuing if you're willing to also question your own deeply held assumptions.

- Everything is up for grabs. Respect the people involved... Question everything else.

For More: Click, The Journey Continues, page 202
- How to Ask Questions That Rock the Boat

HABIT 2
AUDACITY MATTERS
BE AGGRESSIVE WITH YOUR IDEAS AND BELIEFS

"Whenever you think that everything's been invented, or that there's nothing to do because someone else will do it … that's bullshit.

"The amount of things you can do is almost infinite. You shouldn't let anyone tell you that what you're thinking about is a bad idea or isn't going to happen. You should listen to your gut.

"At one point you have to have the courage to take a leap of faith, knowing that the worst thing that will happen is that you will have a hell of an experience and that you will learn a lot."

That's husband-and-wife team of Mariquel Waingarten and Gaston Frydlewski.

At 24, Waingarten disrupted hospitality industry norms when she founded and built the number-one boutique hotel in Argentina. "A lot of decisions in the hotel industry were ancient," she shares. "I wanted to engage the new traveler, one who wanted to have significant stories to tell their friends."

She did no market research. She just trusted her gut. She didn't buy or build the property (as is the norm); she leased it.

She didn't advertise, and instead was bold and aggressive with her own ideas about what would attract guests and keep them coming back. She plowed her limited capital into free hand-made snacks, free Argentinian wine, free laundering services and an Apple computer in every room.

After achieving wide acclaim for her boutique hotel, she then sold it and moved to New York with Frydlewski to pursue their next shared dream. Together they co-founded Hickies, an elastic lacing system for sneakers and shoes.

When asked about making the jump to another venture in a new country, all in the middle of an economic crisis, they said "Extreme situations push you to have extreme ideas and to adapt to survive. Our advice to anyone: This is a moment of change, and you can be a part of it. Open your eyes and ears to the opportunities around you."

This duo exemplify the second successful habit in a disruptive world — audacity matters:

Disruption doesn't flow gently past you.
It rushes in until it is pushed aside
by yet another disruption.
You've got to jump in it to win it.

Audacity Is Simply You Putting Yourself Out There

Whether you're extremely proactive, like these Argentine entrepreneurs, or mainstream proactive, like a typical mid-manager in a typical mid-sized company … to thrive and survive in a disruptive world, you've got to put yourself, your ideas and your beliefs out there.

Not just occasionally. Continuously.

Not Dickensian-style — "Please, sir, may I have some more?" — but boldly. Passionately.

Your own hero's journey begins with the understanding that you've got to be ballsy. Otherwise today's world will drown you out.

"One of the things that's behind everything I do was spending the first 25 years of my life in an economically dying environment, where I witnessed what happens when people fail to adapt to disruptive change. Audacity matters. That's the only way out. Be aggressive with your ideas and beliefs."

That comes from Alec Ross who, for four years, served one of the most powerful women in the world, Secretary of State Hilary Clinton. Ross was Clinton's senior advisor for innovation, a role created for him that blends technology and diplomacy. He spearheaded the 21st-Century Statecraft initiative, digitizing how world leaders and countries interact, and has been named to multiple top-ten lists as one of the big game-changers in politics.

"I am an unapologetic optimist," shares Ross. "The vast majority of people who gave me advice after Hillary Clinton created my role thought that I was crazy. Because of the intractability of many of the issues; because of the deeply embedded culture at the State Department that has been 200 years in the making; and because driving change within a very large hierarchy tends not to be the easiest thing in the world."

So when he says audacity matters, Ross is saying: *Even if others think you're nuts, you've got to believe in yourself and your ideas.* You've got to push past your own doubts, or others' skepticism, and go for it. Draw upon your passion and vision to guide you.

Ross developed his audacity chops years earlier as co-founder of One Economy, a global nonprofit dedicated to erasing the digital divide among third world and lower-income populations.

"We were four guys in a basement and didn't have two nickels to rub together," Ross relayed. "If you want to see people like Bill Gates of Microsoft, you just have to figure a way to do it. I managed to get in front of a lot of powerful and important people who later supported my NGO because I had the audacity to email them directly, hustle my way to get in to see them, and make a compelling case while I was there."

He concludes, "If you have a measure of audacity and a willingness to be aggressive with your idea, that idea has a far greater chance of finding a toehold at the tables of power. You don't need to go rogue. Just be very aggressive about your beliefs and be unabashed and don't necessarily follow the minutia of protocol — that's what's necessary to ascend."

Everyone else's belief in you and your ideas begins with your own. Get aggressive about your ideas. Now.

How to Put Yourself Out There:
Go Inside Who You Are

The first thing you notice about Karla Tankersley is her volume. She laughs easily, big and loudly. Her passions are intense as she jabs at the air. One imagines that she is compelled to live her entire life out loud. Not your typical pocket-protector geek.

Tankersley is a supply chain engineer for Cornerstone Brands, who previously provided LEAN and process improvements for Home Depot, Gap, Kroger supermarkets and GM.

"Engineers can be disruptive," she proudly proclaims. "They can be game-changers, if they choose to be. Amazon and Apple are at the top because of their engineers. I've been able to flip a switch and dramatically change a business. Trust me: You may never read about it in the *Wall Street Journal*, but technical professionals are the ones who kids will be looking up to in the future."

It's Tankersley's past that provides insights into where audacity comes from.

"When I was 12 I lost both my parents. When I was 16, I said 'I've had enough!' I walked into the local judge's chambers and refused to leave until he heard me. I demanded custody of my sister, who's five years younger than me and was placed in different homes than me. It just dawned on me to skip school one day and that there needed to be an intervention. I knew that I had to take charge because no one else was. He gave me custody that day!"

She adds, "Looking back all these years later, that explains a lot of my personality. I'm not afraid to be very disruptive. I will pull the cord and stop the train of progress and say something needs to change. I really think it's because of that experience. It made me strong. I'm a little fearless. It explains a lot about how I act in my life."

Hopefully, you'll never have an experience like Tankersley's. But the lessons she's teaching us are universal: Audacity comes from within you, from your life experiences.

Before reacting to any situation
that calls for disruption,
go inside yourself. Don't just react.
Draw upon your passions and values.

Do Something That Matters With Your Audacity

Jeremy Heimans is co-founder and CEO of Purpose, whose sole purpose is to create global disruptions through social movements. His firm has helped to create movements to fight cancer, change the Australian constitution, stand up for citizens' rights in Sweden and Uganda, and more.

Heimans has been honored with the Ford Foundation's Visionary Award; named one the Top Ten People Changing the World of the Internet and Politics; a Young Global Leader by the World Economic Forum; and one of the Most Creative People in Business by *Fast Company*.

He and Purpose epitomize audacity in action by leveraging the combined power of the Internet and social movements.

"As a child, my mental canvas was the world's biggest problems instead of, like … lunch," he says with a grin.

"When I was a kid, I went around to international conferences and met with Nobel Prize winners and heads of state, and I had this agenda of change I was trying to implement. People didn't know what to make of me, I was such a funny kid. At 12, I had a meeting with the [Australian] foreign minister and at the press conference afterwards I said 'I'm very disappointed with the minister.'"

Heimans is a 21st-century movement entrepreneur, and he encourages all of us to use our audacity to be the same.

"Don't look to institutions to make big change," he pleads. "Maybe the most important way you can create change within institutions is to create something like an innovation team that's protected from the institutional pathologies. The biggest and best value today is being created outside of big institutions." This, coming from an ex-McKinsey & Company consultant.

Be ballsy. Get aggressive. Just make sure you use that audacity to make a difference.

Getting Started ...
1. **Write down** all your reasons and excuses for not being aggressive with your ideas and beliefs.

2. **Give your excuses a Viking's funeral:** Burn the damn list! (See next chapter for more.)

3. **Start being aggressive** with your ideas and beliefs. **Just do it.** You knew how to do it as a child when you wanted something. Just channel the six- or eight- or ten-year-old you.

The only thing holding you back are the excuses you've accumulated since then. And you just burned those!

Audacity Matters: Key Takeaways ...

- Audacity only matters if you use it for something that matters.

- Audacity comes from within you: Tapping into that is what causes others to share your passions.

- Jump in audaciously and ride the wave ... or don't ... and drown with the next disruption. Your choice.

For More: Click, The Journey Continues, page 202

- Career Audacity: Making Big Changes
- Project Audacity: Making Big Pitches

HABIT 3
KILL WHAT YOU CHERISH MOST

YOU MUST KILL YOUR FAVORITE PROJECT BEFORE OTHERS DO IT FOR YOU

In 1997, Clayton Christensen wrote *The Innovator's Dilemma*, the bible on the impact of technological disruptions on companies. Christensen described how disruptive technologies change value propositions within markets, making once-premier products obsolete overnight. The dilemma referred to in the title was if and when senior execs should disrupt their own business before someone else does it for them — because that disruption will happen … fast … hard … without warning … and sooner than everyone thinks!

Christensen's bible focused on *corporate* disruption. An idea that's so '90s and '00s. A quaint era in which corner-office dwellers (supposedly) made all the decisions on workplace disruptions and everyone else's job was to jump when they said jump.

Yes, those suits are still tossing disruptions down at everyone, like hand grenades onto the family picnic blanket. But now we've entered an era of personal disruption. A time during which, even if all the suits in the world did nothing, the disruptions will keep coming. And coming and coming.

This Time It's Personal

"You have to embrace how much things are changing. You have to learn to kill your baby," says this hero.

"That's very hard because you're emotionally attached to this thing that you've built. Yet it's now something that's being disintermediated. You may have built your livelihood on it. You may have defined yourself through what you've been able to build. It's hard, but you have to personally embrace disruption."

Killing your baby is about you disrupting every project you work on — before someone else does it for you. It's about you disrupting whatever accomplishments you're most proud of, and want to protect, before someone else does.

The quote above comes from Bettina Hein, who knows a thing or two about disruption.

"I'm a repeat technology entrepreneur," she proudly declares.

Hein is the founder and CEO of Pixability, which helps businesses increase sales through video. Prior to her current firm, she co-founded and then sold the Swiss-based speech software firm SVOX, whose technology is currently a subcomponent in billions of mobile phones, cars and most every place a computer listens to you. She's also launched START, an organization that advances entrepreneurship among college students, as well as SheEO's, a network for female CEOs and founders of growth companies.

Hein continues, providing both a wake-up call and reassurance for us all: "My function as an entrepreneur is to help birth creative destruction. I think that's a positive thing.

"You can embrace creative destruction if you have a strong core of self-esteem. If you have that you can embrace lots of disruptions, because you know that technology and disruption are just facts of life. They're not you. You are you because you have your values and people around you who share those values."

Five Key Steps

When asked for details about how, exactly, we should kill what we cherish, most heroes gave very similar advice:

1. Accept that you are powerless in controlling disruption from out there. It's going to happen to you whether you participate or not.

2. Make the deeply personal decision to embrace disruption as a given in your life.

3. Continuously conduct inventories of all your projects and the accomplishments you're most proud of, and target those that are most ripe for disruption.

4. Go public with that should-be-disrupted inventory. Declare it openly to your bosses and teammates.

5. Disrupt those projects now … before someone from out there does it for you.

If any of the above sounds similar to a Twelve Step program, that's because it is! Because those programs help people accept things that they cannot change and have the courage to change the things they can. That's what you must do.

Most heroes told us that decisions to kill your babies really isn't about technology or marketplace dynamics or corporate strategies.

It's about deeply personal change and acceptance. It's about your ability to get over yourself, and your willingness to accept that almost-immediate obsolescence is built into every project you take on. And that you need to embrace rapid-obsolescence as a fact of life.

(Inner) Conflict Resolution

Disruptive hero Priya Parker is founder of Thrive Labs and has dedicated her life to conflict resolution. She works with leaders and organizations to zero in on their core purpose, to help them build smarter strategies. She serves on the faculty of the MIT Sloan Innovation Period and Mobius Executive Leadership.

"What I do is disruptive in terms of how people make choices," she says. "I bring together two very different bodies of work. One being internal, in the realm of life coaching or therapy, and the other being rigorous analysis of external forces … And create a space for people to combine the two."

She advises:

"This may seem counterintuitive: Get used to destroying value.

"Most of the people who have not found their sweet spot of confidently knowing their purpose and their abilities are the ones who are very afraid of losing anything that currently has value to them. At an individual level, that's a fear of closing doors and moving on. At an organizational level, it's not wanting to let go of a current source of profits."

As is her nature, Parker gently prods us to get over ourselves and to stop holding on to what is most precious to us. "What I've found is that to make the decisions you need to make, you have to accept that you *will* lose something. Right now, there is a lot of everybody optimizing everything."

Parker closes with the key to disrupting your own projects before others do it for you:

"Those people who move quicker, and are more willing to make trade-offs and lose something that isn't close to their core purpose, are the ones who will ultimately succeed."

Kill What You Cherish Most: Key Takeaways ...

- Get over yourself.
- Be willing to destroy something that is currently valuable to you, in order to create new value.
- Disrupt your projects now ... before someone does it for you.

For More: Click, The Journey Continues, page 202
- Your Projects: Plan Obsolescence From the Start

HABIT 4
DO EPIC SHIT

BE THE BEST IN THE WORLD

"When I returned to Malaysia from New York, it wasn't the best place to launch a business. For starters, it has huge brain drain issues — the smartest people leave the country," says this hero.

"But I really believe in Buckminster Fuller's interpretation of how to change situations: You solve an intractable problem by creating a new model that renders the problem obsolete," says this hero.

"So I decided: Screw that — brain drain will not impact me. My goal is to build *the* greatest place in the world to work — to bring the best and the brightest here. Not *one* of the greatest. The world's greatest place to work. Better than

Google, Facebook, Zappos, better than any other company out there. So I started studying all the things these companies did and decided how to one-up them. Mindvalley was born."

That's Vishen Lakhiani, founder of Mindvalley: a groundbreaking company comprised of innovators, artists, technologists and dreamers from over 30 countries. Mindvalley's mission is to help spread enlightened ideas through 21st-century publishing, media and education.

As a highly successful entrepreneur, there is a method to Lakhiani's madness. He is invited to speak all around the world about building a company culture for today's digitized and disruptive age. Beyond being an advocate for happiness in the workplace and his focus on employee development, Lakhiani's goal is to give away $1 billion to social causes by 2050, through the Mindvalley Foundation.

That's epic thinking. And while many of Lakhiani's goals are outsized and longer term, I wouldn't bet against him. He epitomizes the fourth habit of a disruptive world — do epic shit.

"The best and brightest are now coming here," he continues. "No more brain drain. Over and over again, young people are joining Mindvalley and within a couple years are doing epic things. Get this: Twenty percent of everyone who joins Mindvalley becomes an entrepreneur within two years. That is phenomenal! We're a company that turns our employees into entrepreneurs." (More about that in Habit 12.)

Lakhiani's vision does not stop there: "We asked ourselves, 'What's the craziest, biggest, most epic, mind-blowing thing we could do to serve the world, have fun and make an impact?' We decided to recreate the European Renaissance in Malaysia. We're studying how the Renaissance movement occurred in Florence in the 14th century and we're now applying that to Malaysia. Our goal is in ten years to put Malaysia on the map as one of the top-20 places in the world to start a dot-com company."

Mindvalley has begun this process by opening its auditorium — the Hall of Awesomeness — for free, to people from all over Malaysia. It has become this renaissance's town square for new kinds of discussions and activities — from hackathons to lessons on art and business.

Says Lakhiani, "Malaysians come together in the Hall of Awesomeness to share exciting new ideas, and to say things that are not meant to be said in a mostly Muslim Asian country. To promote dangerous ideas. In short, we are merging a company with a completely free university. We think we can do 10,000 people per year coming here. Now, we're filming the sessions like TED Talks, and we're getting them out to the masses. We call this Project Renaissance. Within three years, we intend to take this global."

Do Epic Shit

Epic, *adjective*: Of heroic or impressive proportions; surpassing the usual or ordinary in scope or size.

Disruptive times call for epic dreams, goals and actions.

Incrementalism and following the status quo results only in career or business extinction.

For Some, Going Small Is the Best Path
For Going Epic

Lots of the heroes we interviewed are like Lakhiani — they are seizing the current era of personal disruption as an opportunity to go big, really big.

If that matches your goals, go for it! There has never been a better time for most anyone to go really big.

But epic thinking and doing epic work does not necessarily mean go huge or go home.

Even big ideas take a lot of small steps done well, with passion, to succeed. Even the most disruptive smartphone app needs somebody to do the hard-yet-very-important stuff behind the scenes. All high-performing teams know that every individual's contribution is crucial to the team's overall success.

Every big and epic idea needs people who are super excited and don't just show up for the daily work, but bring 110 percent all the time.

Sometimes just being boldly you is epic enough.

For example, one service that is being completely decimated by disruptive technology is the U.S. Postal Service. They recently announced no more deliveries on Saturdays. That will only keep the grim reaper at bay for a while. Mail delivery as we know it will soon die a painful death and be completely reinvented.

Mike the Mailman may not be able to do anything about that, yet he still does epic work within his world.

Since 1978, Mike Herr has manned Penn State's on-campus post office. He has had such an impact that people keep encouraging him to run for mayor. Ten years ago, there was a massive protest when a bureaucrat tried to make his playfully decorated walls conform to Post Office regulations. (Fun won. His walls were restored to "merry chaos."). Every year he's the highlight of Penn State's homecoming parade. Every week he has hundreds of students happily waiting on a very long line just to buy a stamp from him or spend time with him; and most everyone brings a gift for him, from cookies to home-grown tomatoes.

Why?

He makes people happy.

Nobody leaves without a compliment or a treat. Students are known to wear special sneakers for him, just so he'll ring his bell and hold up a sign for all to see that says "Nice Sneakers!" Everybody leaves with a smile and warm heart.

Mike the Mailman has no way to change what will happen to the U.S. Post Office. He may even lose his job before he wants to because his boss' boss' bosses don't know how to deal with disruptions (see Habit 12). Yet he is focused on what he can do. Every week he makes a difference in hundreds of people's lives. Within his world, with his own special talents and personality, he is epic — surpassing the usual in highly impressive ways.

You can do epic from wherever you are, with whatever you've got.

Hero Bert Sandie, who is Director of Technical Excellence at Electronic Arts, advises: "Start small. Start where you can actually make an impact. Anybody can do that. There's no roadblock to that."

Priya Parker from Thrive Labs advises: "Don't let a large idea stop you from taking the first baby step."

The Epic Rule of Starting Small

Epic changes always begin with
a first step.

Start within your comfort zone.
Within your sphere of influence.
Allow your epic ideas to catch fire
and grow from there.

But *Never* Think Small

The advice above is classic and timeless. It applies to most
any era. Here's what also emerged related to today's personal
disruption era:

Be the best in the world.

Anyone and everyone can define
how their skills, goals and passions
match specific marketplace needs,
so that there is only one person
in the world who can be the best!

Mike the Mailman did that.

Vishen Lakhiani did that for his firm. He redefined *best
place to work* in such a way (ratio of employees becoming
entrepreneurs, and more) that Mindvalley is the only
possible contender for best.

Priya Parker did the same for herself (previous chapter:
She owns the market niche of consultants who combine
conflict resolution, personal therapy and standard-manage-
ment consulting.)

So did everyone you've read about so far. Whether entrepreneur or employee, leader of one thousand or just one, disruptive heroes skillfully figure out which services they can or will provide, match them to market needs, and then position themselves to be the best in the world in doing that.

That can be as epically grand as the best place in the world to work or the most creative performers/gymnasts/artists in the world (Cirque du Soleil); or as epically personal as the best barista in the world (who would you nominate?) or the best banjo-plucking, paper-bag-playing Appalachian storyteller-musician in the world (David Holt); or as epically heroic as that one first-responder who was there for your loved one in a time of need.

Think Epic, Do Epic

1. Define a set of market needs (established or new) so that you are the perfect match in fulfilling those needs, that also delivers something amazing to the world.

   Market size and goals must be connected to both your dreams (world domination or best in your neighborhood?) as well as your skill sets (if you're tone deaf, it may not be realistic that you'll be doing epic shit as a musician).

2. Deliver.
   Do shit that's epic.

In an era of continuous disruption, everyone can and must start thinking of themselves as the best in the world. And, of course, backing that up by delivering the goods! That's fundamental to all work: great execution.

Because if you're not claiming that title in your niche, somebody right behind you will. You will be disrupted, possibly extinct.

Now More Than Ever: Epic is Needed

As noted earlier, disruptive technologies are reinventing entire industries and how products and services are valued.

And the holy grail is rethinking and then integrating entire ecosystems — for example, how 911 calls, ambulance data, patient histories and doctor's diagnostic tools and blood and organ availability are all interconnected. Reinventing how we save lives.

This is called the Internet of everything and its goal is for every physical thing to be smart: To know its own history (like a bag of peas knowing whether it was refrigerated properly from the processing plant to your stove); And to know your history too (like the Robin Williams bit about his freezer refusing to open because he hit his ice cream limit or being locked out of the Internet because he hit his porn limit).

The era of disruption — both industry-wide and personal — is an era that's dismantling Industrial Age holdovers and recreating them in 21st century form, where everything is smart and talking to every other thing.

"There are so many industries out there that are just old and inefficient," says Garrett Camp, co-founder of Stumble-Upon, the web search engine that built serendipity into your searches and delivers unexpected discoveries. "We're going to have to make things better and solve the most big problems of the world by having more people who will go out there, and not just work at a company, but figure out how they can solve some of these problems."

Camp provides one example by citing another one of his start-ups, Uber. "The old way of getting a taxi cab is so antiquated and heavily regulated. Uber is doing away with all that and disrupting the industry, with a mobile app on your iPhone. You can easily find and book any car available in your area."

Granted … finding a cab is not necessarily one of the world's most wicked problems. But Camp is passionate about joining forces with others to do the same on a much larger scale: "Entrepreneurship can raise the efficiency of entire systems so that you don't have to raise taxes as much because you've taken costs out and increased efficiencies. That impact can be pretty big."

In this time of transition,
the biggest opportunities for
doing epic shit
lie in completely rethinking
how everyday activities are done.

Do Epic Shit: Key Takeaways ...

- Think big (or small!)

- Whether you go big or small
doesn't matter.
Just do epic:
Surpass, bypass and obliterate
the usual ways of doing things.

- Incrementalism equals extinction.
Or, at best, under-leveraged effort.

- Epic journeys always begin with
a first, often small, step

For More: Click, The Journey Continues, page 202
- Redefine Your Niche So Being the Best Is Attainable

HABIT 5
BLOW STUFF UP
CREATE REVOLUTIONARY CHANGES (OR AT LEAST STUDY REBELS AND STEAL FROM THEM)

You can't do epic work without blowing something up.

"To make this point, I used to show a slide of myself next to a ride at Disney World. The sign said 'If you're pregnant or have a heart condition don't go on the ride.' That's *every* ride we're on right now. This is not for the faint of heart."

That's Lisa Gansky, Co-Founder of Ofoto in 1999, a photo-sharing service which was later acquired by Kodak in their attempt to go digital. Shutterfly, which was launched on the exact same day, eventually gobbled up that business. Not for the faint of heart, indeed.

Gansky, like most of our heroes, dances on the leading edge of disruptive change. As author of *The Mesh*, she's now focused on another area that is being blown up by disruption: ownership, the fundamental shift in our relationship with the things in our life.

The idea of full and singular ownership of things creates *a lot* of waste. For example, in North America and Western Europe, we use our cars only 8 percent of the time — yet, for most of us, that car is the second most costly thing we own.

Enter the world of digitized sharing: Zipcar owns a fleet of cars you can share with others, and RelayRides and Buzzcar are peer-to-peer sharing networks, where you can share your own car with others; Pandora, Spotify and others allow us to listen to our music but not have to own it; Airbnb is a community marketplace where we rent our own space to others — anything from a couch to a castle. The list of sharing-not-owning opportunities grows vastly larger every day.

Gansky and others are telling us that this is just the beginning. "Envision," she says, "a partnership between Walmart or Target and thredUP," an online consignment boutique that puts an end to constantly buying kids clothes that will be outgrown within months. That kind of partnership is coming and will completely reinvent buying, consuming and waste patterns.

Whether it's redefining how we think about ownership or education or the arts or war or peace … the era of personal disruption is all about creating revolutionary changes.

Doing epic work includes blowing things up — industries, ways of doing things, people's attitudes — so that you can rebuild anew.

Time for the Big Boy and Big Girl Pants

In today's disruptive world, "there are two kinds of people," says Gansky. "There are the people who are looking for the edge, for what's next. And then there are the people who are holding on for dear life, waiting for the world to stop shaking. Those people are going to wait for a long time."

Since your world ain't gonna stop shaking, you'd better be among the first of those two groups. And if you are, changing somebody else's status quo is part of your job. Blowing up old ways of doing things goes with that turf.

Hopefully, It's in Your DNA:
If Not, Learn From the Rebels Around You

"As a child, my mother had to constantly replace the glass in my windows. I used to blow them out weekly. When I was 10, I learned how to make gunpowder from charcoal and supplies from the pharmacy. I blew up the toilets in school, too. That is who I am."

That is Tiburcio de la Cárcova, Founder of Santiago Makerspace, in Chile. He eventually learned to translate that rebellious childhood, in which he literally blew things up, into a more constructive-yet-still-disruptive way of being.

He's part of the maker movement, which is the open-sourced DIY engineering and manufacturing of computers, robotics and more. Prior to that, he co-founded Atakama Labs, a developer of social games, after selling his videogame firm, Wanako Games, to Vivendi.

"We are in the new industrial revolution," says de la Cárcova. "We are at the beginning of a much more rich, sustainable, generous industrial revolution for inventors and crazy people."

The crazies. If you're not already one of them, you need to study them. Apprentice under them. Hang with them. Learn everything you can from them. Because they are the ones who were born for this disruptive era.

Shortly after his death, everyone at Apple headquarters came together to celebrate the life of Steve Jobs. During that day we heard Jobs' voice, which was originally recorded for a classic Apple ad but never used …

Here's to the crazy ones. The misfits. The rebels.

The troublemakers. The round pegs in the square holes.

The ones who see things differently.

They're not fond of rules, and they have no respect for the status quo. You can quote them, disagree with them, glorify and vilify them. About the only thing you can't do is ignore them because they change things.

They push the human race forward. And while some may see them as crazy, we see genius.

Because the people who are crazy enough to think they can change the world, are the ones who do.

To Blow Stuff Up…

You need to be among the crazy ones…

- Crazy imaginative
- Crazy inventive
- Crazy optimistic
- Crazy rule-breaker
- Crazy visionary
- Crazy enough to believe in your vision… No matter what.

Again:
You Can Go Small to Do Big Stuff

Not far from Makerspace in Santiago, Chile, you will find Matías Gutiérrez, who is Director of Research and Development for Bioquímica.cl. His firm is reinventing how secondary, high school and college-level students experience science education. Through another part of his company, he is also reengineering high-end scientific laboratory equipment to perform at the same exacting standards while costing a fraction of what it would have otherwise.

Gutiérrez shows us that blowing stuff up and completely reinventing how things are done can be done almost at the level of duct-taping things together differently.

"We're trying to change the rules of the game on how scientific equipment is made," says Gutiérrez. "Companies that manufacture new equipment charge a lot of money. For that equipment to get to us at the bottom of the world, researchers end up paying twice as much for it. That makes them less competitive. Due to costs, they cannot be among the first with their discoveries."

He continues, "We recreate the highest-possible-quality scientific instruments, while decreasing costs by as much as 60 percent. For example, for one instrument that detects fluorescent signals, we modified a consumer camera, recalibrated the image-capture to scientific standards, and broadcast the image signal to a larger screen through the researcher's wireless network. We did this locally, without having to wait for components to be imported. That reduced the cost of this instrument from $10,000 to $3,000, and we were able to make it one-third the normal size — saving lab space for researchers is as crucial as saving money."

Gutiérrez is one of many disruptive heroes around the world who are blowing up the rules of how things get done.

We All Can Be Revolutionaries

For many situations, all you need
is MacGyver-like ingenuity,
readily available cheap supplies,
and the drive, determination
and will to upset the status quo.

Like it or not, you are living in an age where part of your job
is to blow stuff up. Own it.

Blow Stuff Up: Key Takeaways ...

- Blowing stuff up* is now part
  of everyone's job description.

- The only limitations are your degree of
  ingenuity, drive and passion for upsetting
  the status quo.

- Be one of the crazy ones.

- If you need to, apprentice under a crazy
  revolutionary: Serve and work with
  someone who is crazy enough to truly
  believe that they can change the world.

For More: Click, The Journey Continues, page 202
- How to Blow Stuff Up and Get Away With It

* Clarification, so no one misunderstands. *Blow stuff up* is a metaphor for positive
creative destruction. This author does not advocate actually blowing anything up.

HABIT 6
BE A TRIAGE MASTER

When was the last time you a) deeply analyzed your ability to look three car lengths ahead, absorbing all that real-time information; b) then assess the speeds and driving patterns of the five or six cars in your immediate vicinity; and c) then were able to describe to someone else why you just *knew* you *had* to hit the brakes a second before a car in the other lane did the same, causing a chain reaction?

Exactly.

It feels to you like you just kind of do it, intuitively.

Yet that's a learned process similar to what you need to learn to master all kinds of disruptions. Those decisions and linked behaviors are a highly complex combination of observing a potential emergency; processing it; analyzing it; accessing all previous driving experiences; formulating a strategy; and executing it — all within milliseconds.

That process, commonplace and frequent for anyone who drives, is a form of triaging — a methodical way of quickly accessing what needs to be done according to urgency and need.

First used in the early 1700s, "triage" comes from the French word for to *pick*, or *cull, or the action of sorting according to quality*. It moved into everyday speech during World War I as an approach to practicing emergency medicine. French doctors in the field developed a quick assessment process:

- Those who were likely to live, regardless of what care they received (OK to delay care);

- Those who were likely to die, regardless of what care they received (OK to withhold care);

- Those for whom immediate care might make a difference in the outcome. (First priority).

Fortunately for all of us, today's EMTs and emergency-room doctors have redesigned triaging for the 21st-century — where that simple three-level assessment is considered primitive.

But the core idea remains relevant to all situations, not just medical emergencies: When quick decision-making is crucial to the outcome, and time and resources are limited and decisions need to be made with limited information — everyone involved had better be skilled in real-time triaging.

Triaging:
The Fundamental Skill for a Disruptive World

In an age of continuous personal disruption, your ability to triage is the one skill that rules all others.

Every day, most of your to-dos are blown up by some disruption. There isn't a single corporate-designed process or rule or tool or procedure that will protect you from instant and unexpected havoc and chaos.

In a world like that, the one skill that rules all others (or that at least jumpstarts all others) is your ability to triage any situation, any time.

Many heroes described how critical this skill is. "It's all about knowing how to quickly make sense of many conflicting priorities and, under intense pressure, pick the right approach," said Julie McCarthy, NPR correspondent, while speaking to us during a break from the war-torn tribal zones in Pakistan.

Part of what won her a Peabody Award, as well as stints in Iran and tracking al Qaeda connections in Europe, were her finely tuned triaging skills. Like you, that ranged from mundane everyday assessments — like quickly tracking down who could corroborate a story — to life-or-death situations if the decision went the wrong way — like whom to trust to safely get her team through hostile territory.

Tim Rowe, who founded Cambridge Innovation Center in Boston, an incubator space that helps entrepreneurs build and launch their disruptive businesses, described triaging in a leadership context: "Leaders need to hold in their minds simultaneously conflicting plans. … Most successful businesses don't end up doing what they started out to do, so the leader has to have the capacity to quickly make 180-degree turns. It's not about having a goal and going after it. It's about a leader and a team who can be flexible as they go on an adventure together."

Rowe spoke of everyone's ability to adjust to the many shifts thrown at them as crucial in this disruptive era.

Whether it's your daily to-dos being changed every few minutes, or strategic plans that are blown up due to a competitor's disruptions — everyone in every organization needs to be able to do in-depth analysis and re-analysis on the fly...

> **Triage:** The ability to assess any situation; rapidly figure out and prioritize what needs to be done and who needs to be involved; and effectively communicate what matters in that situation — many times a day.

For ages, this has been seen as a critical skill for most any leader.

Now, during an era of personal disruption, this must be a universal skill. All of us must be able to triage at a high-performance level.

The Reworking of Work

For over two decades, the Jensen Group's ongoing study, *The Search for a Simpler Way*, has been researching how we get work done. Throughout that time, the need for all employees to be proficient in triaging has steadily increased. This need hit a tipping point in 2012, when study findings declared triaging "the core 21st-century skill for everyone who works."

What forced triaging to be this crucial is an escalating tug of war. At the same time that most every disruption coming at us requires more and more critical thinking, we are also pulled in the exact opposite direction by our ever-shortening attention span — 140 characters are now considered a long story. The level of thinking that most of us do when something crosses in front of us simply is not enough and not good enough.

These two opposing forces are explosively bad in our current knowledge and service work economy. Critical thinking skills are key to everything, and yet our time spent doing that can often be measured in seconds. Another *Simpler Way* finding is that one of the most common behaviors in business today is pushing one's work onto someone else's plate — to get rid of the overload with as little critical thinking as possible!

Becoming skilled at triaging is the way out of this tug of war. Still keeping things moving fast, but doing so in such a way that contains high-level thinking.

During 2011, the Institute for the Future (IFTF) released similar findings. In their *Future Work Skills 2020* report, they identified 10 key skills needed in the future workforce. Seven of which are all components of triage in a disruptive era:

- Sense-Making

- Social Intelligence

- Novel and Adaptive Thinking

- Computational Thinking
  (ability to translate raw data into new conclusions)

- Transdisciplinarity
  (ability to understand concepts across multiple disciplines)

- Design Mindset
  (ability to think differently and design new ways of accomplishing tasks)

- Cognitive Load Management
  (ability to manage all the stuff we have to think about)

The remainder — Cross-Cultural Competency, New Media Literacy, Virtual Collaboration — are drivers of why we all have to get better at triaging.

The Hard Work of Work

Let's return to the field of emergency medicine for additional insights.

Andy Newton is Director of Clinical Operations for South East Coast Ambulance Service in the U.K. He is implementing a new vision for how paramedics assess situations before taking anyone to the hospital — greatly reducing costs while still providing high-level care. He says that improving ambulance services, as well as anyone's ability to triage, "is not rocket science. But we do need to rethink how we use resources and start placing a premium on the effectiveness of upfront assessments.

"The toughest thing about this is that it's just hard work," says this hero. "It requires leaders that understand we need to change how we educate the workforce. Education gives workers the flexibility to be semi-autonomous and still do quality upfront assessments."

You Retraining You

Although Newton is correct — we do need our leaders to radically improve education and training and development — don't hold your breath waiting for that to happen.

It is your responsibility to reskill yourself or update your skills so they include everything on IFTF's list, which emphasizes your ability to triage most any situation. That can be through any combination of:

- Employer-sponsored training
- Hiring a personal coach
- Getting a mentor
- Going back to school
- Or free or fee-based Internet-based training

Here's a simple three-step approach for doing that:

1. Assess:
   Ask for 360° feedback from boss, mentor, co-workers or family on your strengths in the ten IFTF 2020 work skills.

   (Downloadable from Institute for the Future)

2. Prioritize:
   If you need to up-skill, select the one or two 2020 work skills that would have the quickest/biggest impact on your ability to triage.

3. Skill-up:
   Build mastering those skills into your daily routines.

Be a Triage Master: Key Takeaways ...

- Your ability to triage any situation is now the one skill that drives all others.

  It also is an integrating skill — bringing together and leveraging multiple 21st-century skills in scanning, sense-making, understanding, analysis, organizing, simplifying, clarifying and prioritizing ... Super fast.

- Don't wait for someone to re-skill or up-skill you. Take ownership for learning how to triage at the highest level of performance.

For More: Click, The Journey Continues, page 202
- Top Tips: Become a Master, You Must

HABIT 7
MAKE A MESS
FAIL MORE, FAIL FASTER, AND ITERATE, ITERATE, ITERATE

"You have to be accepting of failure," says this hero. "For every initiative and technology that really changes the way IBMers work, we have tons of them that don't.

"We put a lot of stuff out there. We try, fail, and then adapt. *Nobody* is smart enough to say whether something new is going to work or not. We have to watch for what takes off and then adjust accordingly."

That's Francoise Legoues, who heads up Innovation Initiatives for the CIO's office at IBM — focusing on bringing disruptive changes inside one of the world's largest tech giants.

"My job is to understand the technologies and uses of technologies where management will say 'No, this doesn't apply to our business model,' or 'No, this is too scary,' and find a safe way to pilot it to see if it sticks. You need to find a way to try things, even if it looks counter to the current strategy or even if management doesn't understand it."

That's because, she says, "You have to keep challenging the status quo. There may be good reasons for the status quo — 'if it's not broken, don't use limited resources to fix it.' But the problem is that what works now is going to get broken by the fact that the world is moving."

Legoues understands why so many managers fear failure and find it hard to embrace disruptive changes: "The big issue for us now is all-around mobility — how to use whatever you have, wherever you are, whenever you want to, to do your work. Linked to that, though, is a big initiative around security. That's why people are scared — how to keep all that secure." She jokes, "The security people in our organization would like to take all our mobile devices, put them in a vault in a bank, and then say, 'If you have a really, really, really good business reason, you can go and get it.' And what everybody else wants to do is whatever they want to do."

Legoues' role is to help IBM manage the tension between the amazing possibilities that disruptive change can release and all the risks and fears and possible failures that are a part of those changes.

Great Leaders Live the Philosophy of Fail Faster

We interviewed Marissa Mayer at Google, just days before she was tapped to be the CEO of Yahoo. She is the youngest CEO of a Fortune 500 company, ranked number 14 on Fortune's list of America's most powerful business women, and is known for sticking to her values, no matter what. She made as many headlines on the day of her move to Yahoo by announcing her pregnancy and her planned leave of absence as she did for becoming CEO.

Says Mayer, "It's totally OK to fail. You just need to fail fast. If what you've tried is working, throw more fuel on the fire. If not, pull back."

She adds, "I don't think of it as failing. I see everything as an experiment. My goal is to find a way to say 'yes.' We'll try anything once. Then, if something goes wrong, know how to learn from it."

That philosophy is a key part of what got her where she is today. Her early changes at Yahoo received both high marks — Forbes headline: "Marissa Mayer Just Embarrassed Twitter and Instagram with the New Flickr Mobile App" — as well as backlash for some cultural changes: Tackling sagging productivity numbers and trying to emulate Google's dynamic face-to-face culture of teamwork, she abolished Yahoo's work-at-home policy. That did not go over well, especially with Yahoo's younger workers who see working remotely as a given and with working moms had viewed Mayer as their new patron saint.

Like all senior execs, Mayer is also data-driven. What gave her the confidence to make such a move, and to take the heat for it, was analytics. The data from remote workers showed that they were not logging in to work as often as they should have been, which was affecting Yahoo's overall productivity.

As *Fast Company* wrote shortly after her pronouncement, "Whether or not she wants to be a role model for company culture or women in power roles, Marissa Mayer has reinvigorated the debate over telecommuting." In an effort to push Yahoo towards a faster, nimbler culture, Mayer is not afraid to make bold moves and then fix them or change them as the experiment evolves. (More from Mayer in chapters 18 and 19.)

Failing is no longer a problem.
It's an asset — it's the fastest way to learn
and create better innovations.

Most every hero we spoke with said basically the
same thing:

- Launch lots of experiments.
  Pilot new ideas quickly.

- Embrace failure.
  If you're not failing a lot, you're playing
  it too safe — leaving lots of amazing
  possibilities unexplored.

- It's all about how fast you can create
  iterations. Make failure happen faster, so
  you get more feedback faster about what
  works and what doesn't.

If Failing Isn't the Problem, What Is?

While there are amazing exceptions like Legoues and Mayer,
many of us are not getting the leaders we deserve.

In business, too few managers, leaders and companies
walk their talk on failure.

We all hear that we're supposed to *Fail Forward, Fail
Fast, Fail Often,* and then *Iterate, Iterate, Iterate.* Yet how
many business plans or managers or cultures truly endorse
this approach? Many talk about it. But when it comes to
encouraging you to Fail Forward, most managers still opt
for overly managed incremental progress in which even the
tiniest failures are shunned. Risk aversion, especially with

no place to hide if something goes wrong and the decision-maker may look bad, remains the higher priority.

Which leaves most of us high and dry when it comes to truly learning from our failures. Also, if your company is not changing quickly enough, that sets you up for failure! That's not right. Or fair.

So ...
Will You Whine About Others' Risk-Aversion?
Or Are You Going to Do Something About It?

Unless you work for the exceptional manager or company that does give you the space and trust to fail well and fail often ...

> Assign yourself Failure Projects:
> Take on one project per quarter
> (for the more risk-averse ... one project per year) in which you intentionally push yourself or the project beyond a safe and predictable zone.

Failure Projects are not about accepting lower standards or doing poor work.

Instead, they are about giving yourself permission to take yourself out of your comfort zone: Speaking up or pushing back, hard, when that's normally shunned; making decisions where you might look bad if your decision doesn't pay off; taking on the role of disruptive champion and selling a bold move to others.

Embracing more risk on these projects will teach you at lot whether you fail (lessons learned for future projects) or succeed ("See, it wasn't that risky after all!").

Experimenting Is the Best Way to Learn

Tony Haile learned this approach when failure could have meant death. He's now the head of Chartbeat, which provides real-time data analytics to such sites as TechCrunch, Foursquare and Al Jazeera.

Prior to that, he sailed around the world for Team Logica, and, being a glutton for punishment, then joined famed explorer Ben Saunders on several North Pole expeditions.

He compared the lessons learned in fighting 90-foot waves where everyone's lives were on the line to business in a disruptive environment: "What we did in battling the sea and what I do in Silicon Alley are identical…. You launch an experiment. You see how it performs. You review that, and then you start a new experiment based on what you've learned. It's all about being very willing — as a cohesive team — to keep what works, throw away what doesn't and build upon that."

We all need to give ourselves permission to experiment: to keep what works, throw away what doesn't, and build upon that.

Closing thoughts:

"Anything worth doing is worth doing badly …"

— G.K. Chesterton, English writer

"… until you learn to do it better."

— Zig Ziglar, American author, salesman

Make a Mess: Key Takeaways ...

- If you're not failing often, you're playing it too safe.

- Fail fast. In a disruptive world, it's all about how quickly you're moving on to the next iteration.

- Don't just give yourself permission to experiment: If your bosses aren't assigning you to Failure Projects, (those with higher-than-normal acceptance of disruptive risks), then assign them to yourself.

For More: Click, The Journey Continues, page 202
- Start Small Failures, Grow Them Into Big Messes

HABIT 8
DO IT ANYWAY

THERE ARE MASSIVE OPPORTUNITIES FOR THOSE WHO IGNORE "NO"

"When the person who you report to tells you 'No' — if you think that's wrong — you simply don't listen to it," advises this hero.

"Every time I felt it in my stomach — a burning — I knew I had to follow my gut. Once I followed my gut, it was never a question of whether things would work out, it was just a question of how to get there.

"I just had to do the right things for the long-term. Especially in Germany, where people see the problems first, I just had to keep pushing forward. Even when nobody understood my vision."

That's Nora Abousteit. She's describing what it took, as an employee, to convince Hubert Burda Media, one of

Germany's largest media companies, to disrupt its own product line. She was instrumental in rejuvenating one of their print magazines focused on sewing, by liberating copyrights on their patterns and rebranding it as *BurdaStyle*, an open-source pattern and sewing community with over 800,000 members. She also recently founded Kollabora.com, another DIY community, which expanded that vision into jewelry, knitting and more.

Massive Opportunities

In a disruptive world, everything from home crafts to space crafts is up for complete reinvention. There are massive opportunities for those who are willing to take their industry through creative destruction. Abousteit stuck with her gut and pursued her passions in the face of multiple corporate roadblocks.

Her story also illustrates how all the habits you've learned about so far interconnect.

- She questioned everything about how publishing and communities worked (Habit 1)
- She had the audacity to keep pushing (Habit 2)
- She asked a mainstream publisher to kill one of its revenue streams (pattern patents), blow up the way it did things, and try a new model (Habits 3 and 5)
- She's been hailed as one of the best in the world among DIY crafts communities, and she kept her focus narrow in order to accomplish this (Habit 4)
- She triaged constantly and kept trying new iterations of her vision in order to keep things going (Habits 6 and 7)

Additionally, what gave Abousteit the guts to push back on those above her, and to get past the fear of the consequences, was tapping into her inner self — a common thread through all the habits.

She was raised to believe in herself: "I was brought up to keep seeing the possibilities, and to know that I would always be fine." She's half-German, half-Egyptian, and her parents instilled in her a belief that being different is something to be proud of. (A key source of her audacity.) And her business savvy in the DIY world came from spending so much time as a child in her father's workshop and from her family's obsession with crafts.

Important note: Abousteit will be the first to admit that *how* you push back is crucial. "I need to go back to some people," she says. "There are still some scars there." She's working on that.

Especially while being disruptive, people skills matter!

Ask Forgiveness, Not Permission

"I'm fairly well-known for going rogue inside big organizations," says this hero. "Sometimes you have to go rogue.

"Organizations are surprisingly eager for this type of change: People who step up. People who care. Within every organization, there's the great founding passion for the business. And those people always stand out. There's always some rogue band of passionate people who really care about change and enhancing the outcomes of their work.

"Find those people. Band with them. Create a support network of people who care like you do."

That's Caterina Fake, who was once a disruptive employee within big companies, and is now a serial entrepreneur.

Fake co-founded the photo-sharing service Flickr; as well as Hunch, which serves personalized recommendations from the Web; as well as Findery, which provides digital memory posts of all the places you've been. She's also an angel investor, Chairman of Etsy, and serves on the board of Creative Commons.

Of course, saying yes or no is easier now that she's the head honcho. But Fake also has solid advice for middle managers who may not be the ultimate decision-maker: "You have to take care of your people and make sure they are working for their passions.

"You may get orders from above, but your main job is to protect your people from the organization. You have to be the shit umbrella, rather than the shit fan. You create the barrier between them and the organizational crap. You have to make sure that the organization knows that you're fighting for your people. Your job is to protect them from all the organizational hoops they have to jump through. And it's constant — it requires a lot of creativity and skill."

If you work in a big organization, one of the best ways to push back is to be the shit umbrella. Protect your people from organizational crap. That frees them to do their best work.

This is also called providing air cover for your team — protecting them from political fallout as they push boundaries themselves. As Fake says, this is necessary to ensure you're getting great work from everyone: "There's no innovation deficit at large companies. There's no passion deficit at these companies. It's really a matter of helping the organization get out of the way so people can flourish."

> We need to stop confusing conformity with common cause —
> and stop blocking creativity to enforce consistency.

Yes, every organization needs a common vision and common goals and aligned teammates. But after that, especially in a disruptive world, we need to be much more accepting that *how* people achieve those goals will vary and not conform to rigidly designed approaches.

The Future Is a Place Where People Don't Conform

"It's worth considering whether or not you really want to fit in. Find ways to not fit and do things that challenge norms … because that's fun."

That's Nitin Rao, who refers to himself as a leveraged dabbler. His goal is to dabble his way through life in a way that best maximizes the impact of his work. He's co-founder of Sunglass, which has redesigned high-end CAD software, making it cheap and easily accessible in the cloud. He's also founder of the Equal India Alliance and a TED Fellow.

He continues: "Organizations need to be very comfortable with people who don't conform. Even if that means individuals putting their success first and putting the organization second. It makes sense to start with what would excite them."

While that idea may cause some managers to freak out, Rao illustrates why it's so important to take this approach: "Everyone on our team continues to inspire us, versus the other way around. We have a 21-year-old who was initially applying for an internship. He'd already been published in *Wired* magazine, and he did not submit a resume. He submitted an 84-page book about his philosophy of design. He floored us! Not only have I told his story so many times, he shook up the norm of how you apply for an opportunity. I think looking at people like him… we realized that when it comes to company culture and how people get things done, it makes sense to start with what would excite a person like that."

Rao concludes with a warning for those bosses who still want everyone to just do as they're told: "It's tempting, but it's far scarier to be in your own dark room, believing your own ideas and shutting yourself off from the millions of people who can show you what's wrong with your idea."

Crucial Caveat:
The Future Requires Everyone to
Put Their Ass on The Line

Accountability — for everything — matters.

In a disruptive world, there is no place to hide. There are no committees or bureaucrats you can point to while declaring "they wouldn't let me."

There are no excuses. Ever.

There are no silos where you can throw something over the wall and ignore whatever problems remain. No more "that's not my job." Everyone, everywhere is responsible for fixing all problems.

Disruption is an equal-opportunity distribution system. It expects all of us to band together, all the time, to work on whatever is needed.

Borrowing from Spiderman's Uncle Ben: With great power (to disrupt things and not conform) comes great responsibility.

Do It Anyway: Key Takeaways …

- There are massive opportunities
  waiting for those who are willing
  to push past objections,
  and trust their gut more
  when others say "No."

- Another way to push past objections:
  Be a shit umbrella.
  Protect your people from
  organizational crap, so they can do
  more of what matters,
  and less of what doesn't.

- Everyone's ass is on the line 24/7.
  No excuses.
  No place to hide.

For More: Click, The Journey Continues, page 202
- Top Tips: How to Get Away With Doing It Anyway

HABIT 9
GO FASTER
SPEED TRUMPS PRECISION

Simple habit to cover: Go faster. That's it.

Speed trumps ~~presic~~ precision.
(See Habit 7: iterate, iterate, iterate.)

And, oh, by the way:

Once you go faster, go even faster.

Do it ... Done ... Next.

Now, Look at the Person on Your Left.
Look at the Person on Your Right.
The rest of this chapter applies to two of the three of you.
It's up to you to decide whether or not that includes you.

For two out of every three people, the main cause of
slowing things down is themselves. (*Simpler Way* study):

- Ego ...
  "I can't let people see this before it's right."

- Fear …
  "I'll get dinged if it's not perfect."
- Self-Imposed Criteria …
  "I don't have time to think. I have to just keep it moving."
- Excuses …
  "They don't give me the time to think."
- CYA …
  "I can't look bad. What will my boss think of me?"
- Etc.

Sure, there are always some things beyond our control that do slow things down, but the biggest contributor is us … our attitudes and beliefs. An example:

There is a global powerhouse whose products you definitely use. When one travels to their locations in the U.S., China or India, the pace is breakneck. Even in Shanghai, where one would think the Chinese culture of centralized order would prevail, 20-somethings think nothing of leaving corporate meetings to take constant calls from managers or co-workers.

Yet in the Netherlands, the pace seems different. When surveyed, some of their Dutch employees say the corporate culture demands that excessive consensus is built into even the smallest decisions, slowing everything down to a snail's pace.

Upon investigation, the opposite is true. Across the globe, senior execs are working tirelessly to ensure decision-making at all levels is fast and empowered. Still, for some the problem endures.

Why? *Polderen.*

The common usage of that Dutch word means *intentionally slowing things down*. It comes from the Middle Ages where precious land reclaimed from the sea — *polders* — forced independent local groups and municipalities to cooperate in order to maintain the dikes and pumping stations. Even when wars were fought in the region, the two sides still cooperated to prevent flooding — whoever won still needed dry land.

What was once a benevolent way of being — setting aside differences for a greater purpose — now has a *fasterfasterfaster* downside. *Polderen* is used pejoratively in conversations, where consensus-building is used as a delay tactic.

Some of the firm's Dutch employees claim that the corporate culture is too slow because of its approach to consensus-building. Not true. That's what some (of course, not all) of those who were raised there bring with them. They are imposing that approach on the corporate culture.

We Have Met the Enemy and He Is Us

That expression comes from the 1940s cartoon character Pogo. We need to look in the mirror, as Pogo advises.

We need to stop pointing fingers at corporate cultures, or our bosses, or the economy, or, or, or … And we need to start looking at ourselves more.

Delays due to information overload — email, social media, etc. — aren't really the problem. Filtering tools, asynchronous queues, everything you need to get things down to a manageable few items have been readily available for years. The real challenges come down to the choices you make. You can choose to use your tools, time and attention differently. If you give yourself permission to do so.

Delays due to too many wasteful meetings aren't really the problem. You can choose to opt out of many of them, or ask better questions, or participate differently so they're more useful. If you give yourself permission to do so.

Everything comes down to the choices we make. Most every hero we interviewed emphasized this.

One of the main messages sent by the era of disruption:

We have to start making
different choices.
And arrive at those choices
differently than we have in the past.
With different priorities.

That applies to two out of every three of us.

Truly Competitive Speed Comes From Within Us

"Manufacturing crisis schmisis.

"Manufacturing here is not dead. The thing that you can do domestically that you cannot do from China is speed and flexibility. Due to their lot sizes, you've got a four-week head start before their products land here. If you can't beat somebody in a race with a four-week head start, you shouldn't be in the race."

That's Bob Hinty, owner of Hentz Manufacturing and Mark Fore Sales. Hinty was forced to rebuild his businesses and operations after losing his biggest client, Vera Bradley, when they moved much of their sewing and fabrication to China. He's located in America's heartland, in Fort Wayne, Indiana.

Hinty rebuilt based on his firm's ability to solve problems for clients. Several times a week, the plant is working on new ways to make things. Shop-floor employees are regularly pulled in and asked, "How does what you do, or anything you've learned, apply to the problem we're trying to solve?"

Hinty is a firm believer that tapping into the creativity within each employee can solve most any challenge — including speed.

"There is a role for the average guy to say 'I don't like this, and I'm going to change it.' Somebody's going to think about different ways to fuel our cars, and it could be some lathe operator who has had enough," says Hinty. "Most people have a lot more good ideas than they give themselves credit for."

Hinty's vision for where this need for speed is heading next: "Manutailing. Instead of building bigger machines, we build smaller machines designed to manufacture at retail locations. You don't beat a guy by building a bigger factory than him, you beat him through innovation."

His example: "Take shoes … There are only 9 or 10 pieces to a pair of shoes. That's something that can easily be made on the spot. It's just about molding and, in some cases, sonically welding them together. You could laser cut the material at the store and put together a customized shoe in ten minutes, perfectly fitted for that one customer. There are so many opportunities to take advantage of the other guy's multibillion dollar investment and longer lead-times and take them out of the game."

He concludes, "That's how you win the game. You change the rules. If we choose to … we could have manufacturing everywhere, throughout the whole economy, not just in big plants."

For Hinty, like many of our heroes, the next wave of speed isn't about logistics and engineered efficiencies. It's about the choices we make.

Companies, and the executives who run them, as well as every one of us who work, need to begin making choices that include all the realities of a disruptive world.

Many of us have already hit
our threshold for how fast we can go.
The next frontier in speed is freeing
the way we see things,
so we can make completely new choices.

For Two Out of Three of Us, That Means:

The disruptive era must be one
of continuous introspection
and improvement.
Most of us need to unlearn faster
and see things differently faster
than we do now.

The introspective how-tos are *not* the biggest challenge. From journaling to coaches and mentors to personal inventories — one search on Google or Amazon's leadership or self-help sections will yield unlimited advice.

The biggest challenge is how quickly we are willing to see things differently.

Go Faster: Key Takeaways ...

- Speed trumps precision.

- We have met the enemy and he is us:
  The next frontier in speed
  is about how quickly we can
  unlearn and see things differently.

- Why are you still reading?
  In the time it took to read this chapter,
  you could have solved many of
  mankind's most wicked problems!

For More: Click, The Journey Continues, page 202
  · How To Let Go To Go Faster

HABIT 10
LEAP BEFORE THE NET APPEARS
BECAUSE SAFETY NETS ARE FOREVER GONE

"You have to be able to take big leaps without knowing where or how you will land.

"First, follow your heart, then use your brain. See the opportunity, go for it with your passions, then use your brain to figure out how to persist in achieving that goal."

That's Gert Lanckriet, an associate professor at U.C. San Diego, who is currently building Herd It, described as Google for music. His program crowdsources feelings and finds patterns among them — "Is this song romantic? Is this song exhilarating? Which of the following songs makes you feel the same way?" So when you need a tune for workouts or romance or driving, Herd It has already learned from you and others what to queue up.

Like many of the heroes we interviewed, Lanckriet is part of the growing personalization revolution. The entire field of getting to know you, individually, is being disrupted on a daily basis. Many of the things we own and use — from tunes to tutorials, from appliances to apps — will soon be able to completely adapt themselves to you.

Lanckriet typifies leaping before a net appears: "One of the biggest leaps I've taken in my life is coming to the U.S. from Belgium. I just came for the adventure, and to continue work on my master's degree. … Before long, I was getting involved with research and startup companies that had interesting ideas."

Following his passions led Lanckriet to his current endeavor: "Two students were talking to me about their band missing a drummer. I was just learning drums, but jumped at the chance. And while playing music with them, and uploading it onto MySpace, and talking to other musicians about the challenges of being 'discovered,' the idea for Herd It evolved. It all came from several of us following our hearts and figuring it out as we went along. At U.C. San Diego, I reworked my tenure path to fit into what I was doing with music instead of pursuing a more normal path."

We all need to be more like Lanckriet. Rule for a disruptive world:

Don't wait for a safety net.
None will arrive.
Leap first, then build your net
en route.

That doesn't mean being fearless. Everyone is afraid. It's how you push past those fears that counts.

In a disruptive world, most of us will need to make commitments and take leaps of faith without the security or reassurances we wish we had. Because disruptions will always blow up that sense of security.

You may be saving for the recommended cushion before quitting your sucky job. And then six months before you're ready to quit, the company downsizes and you're fired — without the cushion you needed. Or, as an entrepreneur, you may have your angel investors lined up, and the one providing most of your backing pulls out because their business tanked. Or, if you needed to retire during 2009-2012, you were up shit creek without a paddle. Half of what you had socked away was instantly gone due to the market crash.

Safety nets are a thing of the past. They're gone forever.

The People Who Know You Are Your Safety Net

"Risk is not as risky as you think. A strong social network with good people around you is a good enough safety net. If you have that, you can pretty much leave whatever you have and take a calculated risk on anything," says this hero.

"I thought that leaving Goldman Sachs was a huge risk — that if I failed, I'd hurt my chances of going back to it. But I had a lot of awesome people around me, who cared about me, and were invested in me as a person and in my future."

That's Manick Bhan. While he was earning distinguished academic achievement awards in high school, and then pursuing psychology and neuroscience at Duke University, and then doing derivative structuring at Goldman Sachs, there was always one passion for him: music. Specifically, following his favorite bands. That led him to his role as founder and CEO of Rukkus, which offers a new way to stay connected with your favorite artists.

Bhan is not your typical rock fan or dot-com dreamer. He's deeply grounded by his understanding of decision-making, how people work, and — through his derivatives stint at Goldman — the art and science risk-taking. "It's OK to take risks, and it's OK to have someone tell you you're wrong and still stick to your guns," he says.

Beyond relying on your social network as your safety net, Bhan's additional lessons learned: "Being bold and brazen is sometimes the way to go. Don't even think about it. The risk and analytical side of my brain always calculates everything out. The other side says, 'Forget the calculations. Just take the risk.' If you really have a strong vision for the next two or three steps forward, you're not going to get too far off track by going for it."

"Get away from the day-to-day," he also advises. "For three weeks, I did nothing but sit at a white board and sketch out what is now Rukkus. While it has evolved, in many ways it's still the exact same idea. That was like three weeks of boot camp of pure creativity, asking myself: 'What else could we do? What more can we do?' Eventually, there was so much on the board, I realized: 'I can't do all this at the same time, so let's just start here.' Once you have a coherent vision of what the entirety is, then you take it one step at a time to get to your vision."

"When we built our first landing page," Bhan concludes, "it was really just a cookie-cutter template. But I was so excited because I knew we had just completed the first step."

Bhan compared building your safety net en route to a master chess player's strategy: Always staying in touch with the grand vision of how things will turn out, but only taking it one move at a time.

And by taking this approach, what will be your biggest success? Personal growth. Ensuring future successes because you've learned so much.

"Looking at all the things I've done to build this company," says Bhan, "I've grown so much as an individual, that business failure almost wouldn't matter. I know so much more now about how to build a business, how to build a team, and learned skills specific to this field like coding — the increase in what I know and who I know is tremendous. So much so that if Rukkus were to fall apart, with the contacts that I've made, I know there's so much more out there that I can be a part of. I have so many more opportunities now."

1. Do the calculations if you must, but then forget about them. Leap with your heart.

2. Sketch out a Wow vision, then get extremely concrete about the first few steps.

3. Execute every step with the vision in mind, and debrief what you've learned as you take each step.

4. If you measure success in terms of personal growth — that which prepares you for all future leaps without a net — you will never fail.

There Are No Excuses Anymore
Your safety net is you. And those who believe in you.

Leap Before the Net Appears: Key Takeaways …

- Safety nets you used to rely on — in terms of planned security and predictability — are gone forever. They are never coming back.

- Your safety net is you, and the people who believe in you, and your vision.

- In a world with no external safety nets, success will always be measured by personal growth — your improved ability to take the next leap of faith.

For More: Click, The Journey Continues, page 202
- Top Tips: How To Build Your Net En Route

HABIT 11
SIMPLIFY CONSTANTLY

WE ARE ALL IN THE BUSINESS OF FRICTION REDUCTION

Many disruptions are amazingly effective at making things simpler.

Unfortunately, they're also amazingly effective at creating ripple-effect complexities. Sometimes small, sometimes massive, but always a pain in the ass.

For example: It's never been easier to communicate with anyone, anytime, anywhere — *and* information inside companies is now doubling every 500 days, and so much of it is crap.

It's never been easier to create a product, build a company or launch an idea — *and* that means constant churn, competitive nightmares — or worse — for your own product and ideas.

Because all the rules are changing, it's never been easier to do your own thing — *and* all the rules are changing! Every foundation we stand on feels like it's made of quicksand.

And is there anybody on the planet who can figure out airline or cell phone or healthcare pricing structures?!

Disruptions Follow the Exponential Pain-in-the-Ass Rule of Five:

- Minor disruptions bring with them at least five other pain-in-the-ass complications.
  (New form to fill out, new adaptor to buy, etc.)

- Major disruptions bring at least 25 other pain-in-the-ass complications.
  (5x5: new ways of working, new skills to learn, etc.)

- Interconnected disruptions bring at least 625 other pain-in-the-ass complications.
  (25x25: two companies merging their product lines, etc.)

- System-wide disruptions deliver over 39,000 pain-in-the-ass complications.
  (625x625: And that's for a small system.)

And all that pain-in-the-ass stuff is costly. Complexity adds tons of costs to everything. A few examples:

- Complexity adds 15% to 30% in costs to all goods and services. (*Waging War on Complexity Costs*, Stephen Wilson and Andrei Perumal)

- You lose two to four hours per day due to complexity. (*Simpler Way* study)

- Few leaders are effectively dealing with complexity. (IBM study: Almost 8 in 10 leaders expect complexity to increase dramatically, yet less than half feel they're prepared to deal with that increase. Said one CEO, "Most people are looking backward, wishing it was still like it always was.")

Complexity is a serious, serious problem.

Every Disruption Creates Ripple-Effect Complexities

Hero Jimmy Wales co-founded what has become the world's largest encyclopedia, Wikipedia. For him, the joy was in the journey: "I always try to do the most interesting thing I can on any given day," says Wales. "Even in the times that it wasn't clear that Wikipedia was going to be a massive success, it was fulfilling in and of itself. It was fun!"

That one disruption — open-source contributions, where everyone volunteers for the greater good and everyone is involved in vetting each other's work — has been used as the model for amazing changes far beyond Wales' original vision. For example, TED, MIT, Harvard and others have used the model to create open-source classrooms where students help grade each other's work and educators freely share and use each other's materials.

Major upside changes from that one disruptive idea!

But for every upside, there's also the blowing up of Encyclopedia Britannica and an entire print-based reference industry; and all those educators and institutions that need to completely rethink how they compete and excel. And the success of that disruptive idea also means that free is the new norm — entire industries need to rethink how they make money because so much of what they used to charge for is now available for free.

The Only Way Out:
We're All Responsible for Simplicity

Complexity and friction — how hard it is to get stuff done — are the unfortunate side effects of most every disruption. A new app or a new way of shopping may make one thing simpler, but it also causes friction and pain-in-the-ass changes somewhere else.

That means that simplicity is now a job for all of us.

Here are a few steps we must all take, based on more than two decades of research from the *Search for a Simpler Way*:

1. Embrace building simplicity as part of your job.

   Don't wait for *them* to fix something. If there's a pain-in-the-ass complexity in your workplace, put your ass on the line to make it easier, simpler.

2. Start simply: master clarity.

   The need for making things clear, understandable and useful is huge! And everybody can do it, every day.

   In today's disruptive world, the hardest part of work is the ability to order, make sense of, and connect everything demanding our attention … how we create clarity. How you organize and share what you know really matters!

   Everybody who works should know how to create a great one-page summary, and get to the point in 30 seconds or less. (Three seconds electronically).

   Everybody who works should be able to quickly ask clarifying questions to see if there's a difference between what the other person *wants* and what they *need*.

3. Do not accept suckiness as your problem. Be vocal in pushing back, or create workarounds. Most workplace rules, tools and processes still suck. Most of them make things simpler for the company, but overly complicate

your work and your life.

(See Habit 17)

4. Always put yourself in the other person's shoes.
Ask: "Did I make this easier for you?"
In a disruptive world, that's a most desperately needed service!

Simplicity Is Human-Centered

True simplicity is always centered on the needs of the person you serve — the user, the customer, the patient, the audience.

One of the best companies in the world at doing this is the design firm IDEO. They have designed everything from the first mouse for Apple to homes for wounded warriors, to entire school systems in Peru, to heart defibrillators and surgical instruments — all by working backward from the needs of the end-user.

IDEO's founder, David Kelley, spoke about what's core to the company's approach during a recent *60 Minutes* interview: Be "empathetic to people. Try to understand what they really value."

IDEO has built, and offers for free, a Human-Centered Design Toolkit. Their three-step process will *always* yield simplicity for the end-user. Because it begins with desirability — what people want and need:

- Hear and immerse yourself in the needs of the people you serve.

  Most of us solve problems from our own perspective. To make anything simpler — from how you write emails to how you serve customers — you need to live in the other person's world for a while.

- Create innovative approaches to meet those needs and exceed their dreams.

  A lot easier once you've walked a mile in their shoes.

- Deliver great solutions by continually making them better.

  Iterate, iterate, iterate!

Back to Personal Responsibility

"I see a world where my firm no longer exists. Everyone will and should soon be able to do what we do."

That's Jake Porway, founder of DataKind, whose mission is make data easy to understand and use. DataKind helps nonprofits and NGOs like the Grameen Foundation and the United Nations make sense of the data they've collected and then communicate it in compelling ways.

Given the rate at which information technology is advancing, Porway envisions a world in which even grade schoolers will soon pull patterns and stories from big data, rendering his firm's current offerings extinct. The same fast growth of info-tech will also further complicate issues such as privacy, information security and intellectual property rights.

The trend is unstoppable and will only intensify: All disruptions will continue to make some things a lot simpler, as well as dumping lots of other complications back onto us.

The only solution is for each of us to take personal responsibility for making things simpler. For ourselves and for those we serve.

Simplify Constantly: Key Takeaways ...

- Simplicity is now a job for all of us. We're all in the business of simplification and friction reduction.

- Start simply. Master clarity.

- True simplicity is determined by the needs and dreams of the people you serve. To do it well, walk in their shoes.

For More: Click, The Journey Continues, page 202
- Five Ways to Make Most Anything Simpler

Unless otherwise noted: All data cited in this chapter is from *Simpler Way* study.

HABIT 12
HAVE LOTS OF AFFAIRS

(ON YOUR BOSS)
EVERYONE MUST BE AN ENTREPRENEUR

"More and more people are going to require the freedom to work on their own projects while they're under the employment of somebody else. Freelance projects. Businesses on the side. Pursuing their own ideas.

"With our employees, we've always looked at their side jobs as continuing education. What they learn on those projects, they bring back to us. Employers need to understand that in order to keep tomorrow's employees, they're going to have to loosen their clutches."

That's Jude Goergen, a creative team member at SBN Interactive, a Cleveland-based multimedia firm focused on the intersection of digital music, graphics and production services. SBN's goal is help its clients do disruptive things

— such as helping E3 Clean Technologies get the funding it needed to turn wastewater (piss) into drinking water.

The idea of employees having side businesses, or building their portfolio through freelance projects, has always been a mainstay of creative industries like design, music and film, as well as in businesses where the work is easily mobile, such as landscaping, bookkeeping or hairdressing.

In a disruptive era, every employee — the creative types as well as lathe operators, forklift drivers, process engineers, hotel managers, cashiers, warehouse pickers — everyone must also be an entrepreneur.

Even if you don't want the hassle or responsibility of your own business … Doesn't matter. You must also be an entrepreneur.

Even if you work for a manager from the Dark Ages who expects 110 percent of you all the time. Doesn't matter. You must also be an entrepreneur.

The Kiss of Death
Depending only on a paycheck.

This includes multiple paychecks, such as holding a second or third job. If all your earned income is as someone else's employee, you are among the walking dead.

In a disruptive era, being someone else's employee is the riskiest job within the civilian sector. For example: In 2002, in the U.S. 100,000 white collar jobs were moved offshore. By 2015, that number is projected to be over 3.3 million. And even if the average job tenure lasts three years or more, career planning is a joke and life planning is a mess. Every employee lives with the daily anxiety that today might be their last day on the job — and that the only thing they can control, their performance, has little to do with whether or not they keep or lose that job.

Job security through a paycheck is a thing of the past. We all know this, yet far too many of us keep ignoring what we know.

The only job security is within us.
Within our ideas and skills.
Within our next idea and our ability to learn.
We need to kick our addiction to paychecks.
Everyone must be an entrepreneur.

Lessons from an Everyman

"The biggest lesson I've learned is don't give up. Don't ever give up. No matter what you do in life, including your hobbies, expectations from your life, and the serious decisions you need to make … don't give up. There are always different routes for you to accomplish your goal.

"But in order to get to the don't-give-up state, you need to start something. If you don't start, you don't have anything to give up."

That's Cenk Karasapan. He's one of our heroes not because he invented a disruptive product, or built a dot-com company or has a big social network following.

Karasapan is an everyman hero.

He's just one of the many millions of people who do whatever it takes — disruptions be damned. Until he was 30, much of his life was dedicated to taking care of his mother and brother in his homeland of Turkey. Then his yearning to continue his education brought him to America. His strategy of don't-give-up was tested on the flight over —

his plane, like many others that day, was turned back as U.S. airspace was suddenly closed. That was on the morning of 9/11.

He eventually made it to the U.S., and he persevered. He learned English as his seventh language. He and his ex-wife lost their only child. He finished a dual-major university degree. Throughout it all, he has lived a blended life of employee/entrepreneur:

- Shoe salesman at Sears, Kansas City, Missouri
- Hotel sales associate
- FedEx driver

During each of the above, he saved enough to:

- Purchase a FedEx franchise
- Sell the franchise
- Start his own limousine service
- Sell the limo service
- Move to New York City

He is now a regional accounts manager for AxelaCare Health Solutions. While still at that job, he is also launching a new business.

Karasapan's advice for successfully leading a blended life of employee and entrepreneur: "Don't give up your dreams. Once you're on the road, you go. If there are 50 doors, and you're on the 48th door and get tired, do you give up? No. You keep trying."

1. The only thing you really need is drive.

You may have a big idea, or you may not.
You may have a great product, or you may not.

But every successful entrepreneur has one thing in abundance — drive.

Don't wait for the big idea or right opportunity.

Do start your own business or find a partner. Now!

If you are an entrepreneurial or freelance virgin, check out elance.com or oDesk.com or *The Freelancer's Bible* by one of our heroes, Sara Horowitz, to start educating yourself as to what's possible.

Lessons From a Trustafarian

Dickie Haskell may seen like an odd choice for a chapter on entrepreneurship. A self-described *trustafarian*, he squandered his family trust money and has lived off the monetary grid for more than six years — homeless, dumpster diving, house squatting, and surviving off the waste of society.

He's just now making amends with his family, and has turned his knowledge of how much we all throw out into multiple composting businesses — bartering his services for whatever he needs. Wherever his nomad life takes him, currently Los Angeles, the legacy he leaves behind is a community garden.

While he has traveled a different road, his insights and wisdom are equal to that of any entrepreneur. Like Waingarten and Frydlewski (page 24), and Bhan (page 85), he talks about the universal traits that make for great entrepreneurs, great employees and great people:

Haskell: "Everybody has to discover their pitfalls on their own. We need to know why something doesn't work in order to own that experience. I've chosen all the things that have happened to me. I can't point fingers or say that somebody else has caused me to not be able to achieve my fullest potential."

2. One of the connections between being a great person, a great employee, and a great entrepreneur is accountability for achieving your highest potential.

If you let it, your business or product will take you on a journey where you are the best you that you can be. To ensure that happens:

Don't ever evaluate entrepreneurial success solely on monetary or business terms. Every entrepreneur we interviewed said true success was their personal growth — working on something they were passionate about, and learning from failures — as well as their enhanced ability to make a difference.

Haskell: "I think it's healthy to be able to interact with multiple economies. For me, that has been moving fluidly between barter economies and the regular commercialized economy. Using all aspects of our economy is really important."

3. You will learn more about monetary success in one year as an entrepreneur than you could in a lifetime as an employee.

Don't risk too much. It's OK to stick your toe in the water before you jump in with both feet.

Do risk smartly. The biggest challenge for most start-ups is cash-flow — too much going out, not enough coming in. Borrow from family, work out of a closet, improvise. Also use online communities heavily. They have a lot to teach you!

Haskell: "Try something. Don't get too attached. If what you're doing is not giving you inspiration, then it's probably not your life's work. Move on and try something else. Ultimately, if you don't find work that inspires you, I don't think you can achieve satisfaction out of life. My dad thinks that everybody has to just suck it up, and stick to a job even when they don't want to. I adamantly disagree."

4. Never just suck it up.
   If being a full-time entrepreneur
   is not for you, then have lots of affairs
   on your boss. Living the blended life
   of an employee/entrepreneur is a
   great way to pursue your life's work.

Now Is the Time!

Dr. Muhammad Yunus, founder of the Grameen Bank in Bangladesh and partner to one of our heroes, Saskia Bruysten, has said: "All human beings are born as entrepreneurs. But unfortunately, many of us never had the opportunity to unwrap that part of our life, so it remains hidden."

The time has never been better to unwrap that part of your life!

Have Lots of Affairs: Key Takeaways ...

- If all your earned income is as
  someone else's employee, you are
  among the walking dead.
  Start your own business. Now!

- The only thing you really need is drive.
  Big ideas or an innovative product
  or angel investors are great,
  but not necessary.

- Job security comes from within you.
  If your startup comes from in there,
  you will create all the security
  you need.

For More: Click, The Journey Continues, page 202
- Getting Away With Lots of Affairs (On Your Boss)

HABIT 13
GO BACK TO THE FUTURE

Two sources emerged as disruptive heroes spoke about whom they turn to for advice and mentoring:

The wisdom of age and the wisdom of the age of disruption.

Both. Dancing together as yin and yang.

Those Who Have Been There Before You

"I work with people now who say, 'You worked with my grandfather.' I'm in the business of teaching as well as creating. Inspiration has got to be passed on to others," says this hero.

He learned that from his mentor: "One of my early bosses changed how I see everything. He was inspirational, sophisticated and sensitive.

The work he did was extraordinary, and I love the way he led people. The way he would fight for his creative people."

That's Bob Giraldi, one of the original *Mad Men*, who played a starring role in advertising's Golden Age. In addition to directing over 4,000 commercials, he also set the tone for music videos in the early days of MTV — his unique storytelling skills were first seen in Michael Jackson's *Beat It*, Pat Benatar's *Love is a Battlefield* and many other videos.

"When I became a director, I realized that I was in a business that was at the forefront of shaping pop culture. Then my videos began to contribute to changing the way America sees itself," says Giraldi. Many of the cutting-edge videos currently on YouTube and social media have their ancestral roots in his work.

Giraldi candidly admits that none of that would have happened ("I'd probably have grown up to be the owner of a gas station") if it weren't for one person who wisely pointed him in a different direction.

Giraldi was admitted to college on baseball and basketball scholarships. The athletic director called Giraldi just before he was to arrive on campus and said, "I'd love to have you here, but your aptitude in art is extraordinary and this school doesn't go near that. However, my brother teaches at Pratt Institute, a great school for art, and they have two open athletic scholarships. You should go there."

That advice changed the course of what many of us would see, feel, hear and experience thereafter.

Mentors matter.

They can change the course of your life,
which means forever changing
the course of every life you touch.

We asked every hero "What makes you … you?" Most every
one began with their parents or family.

Management guru Don Tapscott spoke of discussions
around the dining room table. "I remember them being
deeply, deeply unhappy about war and unjustly treating
others. … Civil rights. … Fairness. … Women's rights."

Social media investor and guru Lisa Gansky learned a
lot about what she does now from her Russian grandfather,
who was in the restaurant business in Philadelphia: "He had
no formal education, but spoke nine languages. Because
he was fluent in the languages spoken in their kitchens,
he ended up coaching business owners and their staffs. He
built incredible relationships with them and became a seed
investor in many of their businesses."

Our family and our upbringing will always be one of the
biggest influencers of where we go and what we do.

Beyond that, once we're out on our own, making our
own way, there's always at least one person — like Giraldi's
athletic coach and his early boss and lifelong mentor, Steve
Frankfurt — who either changes the course of our lives, or
gives us the guidance we need to truly find ourselves.

In a disruptive era, we need mentors who
share the wisdom that comes only with age,
with hard-knocks — those who have already
experienced what we must also learn.

And then there's the wisdom of youth. … The wisdom of
"Rules?! What rules?"

Those Who Go Where No One's Gone Before

"It is not a coincidence that so many of the breakthrough innovations are being developed by 20-somethings. Everyone who grew up as digital natives are hard wired for this. If you really want to be able to harness innovation, if you really want disruption to be something that works for you, you've got to connect with, empower and learn from people who don't have the right resume or the right experience."

That's Alec Ross, former Senior Advisor for Innovation to Hillary Clinton. It's no coincidence that all our heroes either are young, or spoke passionately of the need to learn from and empower today's youth. The combination of digital natives (mid-20s or younger —who know nothing but an Internet- and apps-driven world) with a boundless passion for innovation is a key driver of today's disruptive era.

Don Tapscott is one who knows this all too well. He's been called one of the most influential management thinkers of our time. He has been guiding us through today's disruptions and the power of digital natives through his books *Paradigm Shift*, *The Digital Economy*, *Growing Up Digital*, *Wikinomics* and *MacroWikinomics*.

Tapscott pulls no punches when speaking about our current situation: "Tinkering and incrementalism are insufficient. Many of our institutions that have served us well for centuries are at various stages of atrophy and failing, and we need to rebuild them around new technologies and new principles. We need to change the deep structure and architecture of every institution. We need to rebuild them around the principles of collaboration and openness and integrity and interdependence. That's a tough message for leaders of old paradigms."

Tough love. Tapscott is a firm believer in disruption.

He also believes that today's digital natives are the ones who can take us where we need to go. During a recent commencement speech, he charged them with that role: "By all means, go and work hard and be prosperous. … Live a good life. … But we need more from you than that. The world is broken, and we need you to provide leadership for transformational change."

> In a disruptive era, we also need mentors who will shake and shape our future — the younger generation who have no stake in preserving the status quo.

Get Two Mentors:
Half Your Age and Twice Your Age

The process is no different than what you already know. You're just adding someone to the mix who will take you places you normally wouldn't go.

1. Know thyself.

   Ideally: Both mentors will help you with everything — just from two different perspectives. If you need to work on your addiction to risk-aversion, that's definitely the place to leverage your half-age mentor.

2. Contract with your mentor.

   Especially with your half-age mentor, get task-oriented assignments. Build a business or a project, or pull together a team, in the way a digital native would do it. For places you've never been before, you can only learn by doing.

Don't think that asking your 12-year-old nephew for tech advice is the same as mentoring. It's not. Mentoring is not about tech proficiency, it's about your mindset, your way of making decisions, your growth as a person in a disruptive world.

3. Do epic stuff.

At some point, both your mentors will have invested a lot in you. You owe them a great ROI. Not monetary. You owe them personal change. Do even greater work with what they taught you!

Go Back to the Future: Key Takeaways ...

- Get two mentors:

  One twice your age, who will share with you wisdom that comes only with experience.

  One half your age, who will take you where no one's gone before.

- Joyously dance with both. Integrate both sets of wisdom into a new path forward.

For More: Click, The Journey Continues, page 202
- Five Dos and Don'ts With a Half-Age Mentor

HABIT 14
FIX THE WORLD'S FLYING TOILETS
FIND SOMETHING MORE IMPORTANT THAN YOU, DEDICATE YOUR LIFE TO IT

"In the slums of Kenya, eight million people resort to a practice known as flying toilets — open defecation in plastic bags and then tossing the bags onto the side of the road.

"They do this because no better options are available to them.

"We are trying to address this by building a dense network of low-cost sanitation facilities throughout the slums."

That's Lindsay Stradley and David Auerbach, MIT MBAs and co-founders of the Sanergy project — whose objective is to build a new sanitation infrastructure in the slums of Nairobi. Once their model is proven, they hope to then take it global to other urban areas with similar needs. Each toilet is operated by local entrepreneurs, and Sanergy collects the waste, converts it into bio-gas, fertilizer and electricity

— which creates sustainable funding for the project and payments to the owner/operators.

Since launching operations in June 2011, Sanergy has become the largest provider of hygienic sanitation in the Mukuru district of Nairobi — safely removing over 500 megatons of waste and creating 250 jobs within that slum.

Stradley and Auerbach will be the first to tell you that — as in many large-scale changes — their biggest challenges aren't in building the actual infrastructure, but in creating a community of champions who want and will support those changes. "One woman became a champion because, especially at night, most women leave themselves open to sexual assault in their trip to and from a toilet," Stradley shared. Such attacks would be prevented with the new and well-lit Sanergy locations. "She was also excited to become a toilet owner/operator because income opportunities are so rare for the women in her slums."

"Alan, who is 10 years old, was at one of the schools where we were piloting the use of the toilets. He quickly became the ambassador to the other students," says Auerbach. "He blew us away, not only with his ability to communicate the importance of sanitation to his fellow students, but he also enforced good behaviors … like not throwing rocks in the toilet and waiting your turn in line. This taught us the importance of working with kids Alan's age. For this idea to take hold in their society over a long time, children will be the main champions."

The Secret of Happiness in a Disruptive World: Yours and Everyone's

The world is filled with tough, intractable and systemic problems, like flying toilets, which are fixable only if enough of us step up to help. And stepping up isn't just important because we all live on the same blue sphere. It's important to your own happiness.

This chapter's subtitle — *find something more important than you and dedicate your life to it* — comes from philosopher Dan Dennett during a TED talk titled "Dangerous Memes." His dangerous idea: The secret to true happiness is dedicating ourselves to something bigger than ourselves. To an idea. A cause. A need. A set of values or principles. Or to others, those we know and those we don't.

This is *super-critical* during an era of disruption.

Many of the things we depend on — a stable job, a stable economy, our savings being there when we need them, etc. — are going to be forever subject to turbulent and constant change, whether we like it or not.

Yet no matter how much gets disrupted …

The things that are bigger than ourselves — family, love, community, making a difference, values, principles, causes — are what will keep us grounded …

… providing a solid foundation underneath us when all else feels like it's coming apart.

During times of disruption, dedicating ourselves to something bigger than ourselves is key to our happiness and a whole lot more.

Many of our heroes described how this approach helped them ride any wave of disruption and come out better on the other side.

Something bigger comes in many different forms. For Auerbach, fixing the world's flying toilets is part of being of service to others: "In 2006, I returned from two years of teaching in China to go to a family reunion. There were 70 family members there, and not a single person was working for a for-profit corporation. Every person was working in some way towards a social mission, either as an educator or as a public servant. That really got me thinking: My background is driven by the need for social justice. What I've learned, through my work with the Clinton Foundation and others, is that economic justice can be married to social justice."

Marissa Mayer proved that family was bigger than herself, and Yahoo, when she announced her pregnancy and planned leave of absence on the same day she became Yahoo's CEO.

For Deepa Narayan, an international poverty advisor, it's her spirituality: "When we were growing up in India, every Sunday my father would read from the great religious traditions. From books on Hinduism, the Torah, the Qur'an, the great Sufi poets. What stuck inside me is being dedicated to tolerance and respect for others."

The simple belief that anything is possible can also be that bigger-than-ourselves idea. Many heroes had the same belief as Bethany Henderson, founder of City Hall Fellows, whose mission is engage the youth of cities in becoming effective change agents and community leaders. Says Henderson: "I don't like taking no for an answer. Whenever I see a challenge, especially where a change would be really impactful, I'm always looking for ways to short-circuit whatever obstacles there are."

Find something more important than you and dedicate your life to it.
It can be save-the-world big, or a simple guiding principle.

You can do it from your current job, or you can make a career switch.

No matter how you choose to pursue it, here's the effect it will create ...

The bigger the challenge, or the more deeply held your conviction, the happier you will be, and the easier it will be to ride through any disruption or to create your own.

We're All in This Together

For five years, Saskia Bruysten was a senior consultant for the Boston Consulting Group. Her role was to advise senior execs on business strategy. While she really loved her work and the firm and their clients, something continued to gnaw at her. "Why am I doing this? Is optimizing shareholder value the best way I can make a difference?"

Asking those questions eventually led her to co-found Yunus Social Business with her partner, Nobel Peace Prize Laureate Professor Muhammad Yunus. Their firm helps companies and NGOs run businesses that both turn a profit and reinvest some of those profits to address specific social needs such as poverty, healthcare or education.

"What will help," she says, discussing making a difference, "is everyone looking at their neighbor and finding out what problems other people have. Both in your neighborhood and further away, in developing nations.

"There have been several waves of change over the last few years," she continues. "And one of them has been the focus on individualism — giving you, as one person, the absolute freedom and tools you need. ... All the I-focused things we have ... I think that's one of the things we should question once in a while. Despite the fact that two-thirds of all people live on less than three dollars a day, many of us forget that because that's not part of our daily lives."

Bruysten concludes: "Paying tax monies and giving a few donations here and there is not enough anymore. Maybe the answer is for all of us to create our own social initiative, in whatever way we can."

Getting Started

Most heroes said that finding something bigger than you and dedicating your life to it is a very personal journey — there is no cookbook set of steps. However, they did provide a few guidelines:

- ## Choose one thing and really focus on that. And aim high.

  Don't try to boil the ocean. Don't try to address more than you have the time and energy for. Focus on one flying toilet issue that you deeply care about, and where you can add the most value. But when you go after it, aim high! Truly make a difference!

- ## Focus on inequality.

  In all areas — earnings, access to clean water or a good education, or technology, or a safe environment — increases in disruptions means greater and greater gaps between the haves and the have-nots. It's up to each of us to address those gaps in our own way.

- ## Accept that your passion and your income may not be the same.

  This is why so many of us address flying toilet issues and how we make a difference through volunteering.

Fix the World's Flying Toilets: Key Takeaways ...

- Finding something more important than you and dedicating your life to it is about more than personal happiness and making a difference.

  It is the solid foundation we each need when disruptions constantly shift the ground under our feet.

- Find the flying toilet problem that matters most to you, and dedicate yourself to fixing it.

For More: Click, The Journey Continues, page 202
- Top Tips: Making a Difference

Don'ts

THINGS TO AVOID

4 HABITS FOR ENJOYING THE RIDE

Damn everything but the circus!
… damn everything that is
grim, dull, motionless, unrisking,
inward turning,
damn everything that won't get into
the circle,
that won't enjoy,
that won't throw its heart
into the tension, surprise, fear
and delight of the circus,
the round world, the full existence …

~ e.e. cummings

HABIT 15
DON'T FIGHT STUPID

FIGHT *FOR* THINGS, NOT AGAINST OTHERS' PROBLEMS

"Don't fight stupid. You are better than that. Make more awesome.

"If you are trying to make a difference, to make something happen, and you keep bumping into 'No' … no one who will say 'Yes,' no process that will help you, no appeals … you are going to have a long, slow, painful death," advises this hero.

"Get out of there! "Every time I tried to win over stupid, I regretted it. And every time I moved on, I was glad I did. Don't fight stupid!"

That's Jesse Robbins, who earned the title "The Master of Disaster" for translating his emergency preparedness as a Seattle volunteer firefighter to Amazon's back-room operations. His role was to triage and fix emergency incidents in Amazon's server centers and tech infrastructure.

"My operations experiences at Amazon had a lot of parallels to fire fighting," he shares. "You don't build the buildings, but you're responsible for putting the fires out quickly when something happens, and going to great lengths to minimize the damage."

Robbins is now co-founder of Opscode, a firm that creates open-source solutions for those back-room needs. Even though his leadership role in Opscode occupies most of his time, he still serves as a firefighter at Burning Man, the annual alternate-universe event in the Black Rock Desert.

Robbins' advice for all disruptive change agents draws upon his triaging experience and more:

- **Take Improv Lessons:** "One of the things that's made a giant difference in my success is that I've done a lot of improv theater. It teaches you to instantly go with anything that is thrown at you, always responding positively … always building upon what was handed to you."

- **Give Others Change Tools:** Give them whatever they need to be your champion — metrics, talking points, anything they need.

- **Leverage Compelling Events:** When something bad happens to the organization, that's when people are most ready to try new things.

He learned the lesson about Never Fighting Stupid whenever he did try to win that fight: "I've never looked back and said, 'I was right and they were wrong and I'm so glad I won.' On the other hand, every time I've gotten a chance to build something new with great people, I remember every single one of those. If the organization or your boss is incapable of changing, it's time for you to move on. There are a host of opportunities waiting for you elsewhere."

Organizational and leadership stupidity are rampant.

If you find yourself fighting an uphill battle, move on. Quickly.

In a disruptive world, there are far too many other opportunities waiting for you. Never waste your time or energy fighting stupid.

Fight for Things

Jan Boelen is Artistic Director of Z33, a Belgian art and design firm, and chairman of the Flemish committee for Architecture and Design. We caught up with him mid-2012, shortly after he and two other heads of masters programs resigned from Design Academy Eindhoven, one of the most influential design schools in the world. All three had major differences with the academy over the changing role of design in society.

"In the end, it became clear that we were in the irrationality of rationality," he says. "We could no longer defend the Academy's policies to our teams and to our students.

"The turning point for me was the moment I realized I was fighting against something, and not *for* something. Then, I needed to leave. I would advise everybody to continually determine whether you're fighting *for* something or somebody — whether you believe in it and can defend it. If you can't, your motivation and energy stops."

Fighting *for* something is …

- The moral courage and will to take a principled stand.

- Speaking difficult truths: Driving a conversation that many wish to avoid.

The moment you realize that fighting for something is no longer possible, and that circumstances keep forcing you to fight against things, is the moment to decide to leave.

Thrice Stupid, Then Leave

Sure, we all have to endure *some* bureaucratic and leadership stupidity. That goes with the turf. Beyond that, several of our heroes mentioned the Rule of Three …

1. First Fighting Stupid: A misunderstanding?

   Give the other party the benefit of the doubt. Maybe what looks stupid just requires a little more work in creating a shared understanding.

2. Second Fighting Stupid: A pattern is emerging.

   The second time you run into a major decision or policy that you know is stupid and that you can't defend to your team, start scrutinizing how much more stupidity surrounds you and others.

3. Third Fighting Stupid:
   Where's the door?

   Depending on your situation, maybe this means
   only beginning your search for a new job, and not
   an immediate departure. But if you're still there six
   months to a year after the third major incident of
   stupidity, then you're part of the problem. You have
   become somebody else's Stupid to be fought.

Don't Fight Stupid: Key Takeaways ...

- Don't fight stupid. Ever.
  You are better than that.
  Make more awesome.

- Thrice stupid:
  Get out of there!
  In a disruptive world, there are lots
  of opportunities waiting for you
  to make that decision.

For More: Click, The Journey Continues, page 202
- Five Ways to Spot Stupid

HABIT 16
NEVER HESITATE

FEAR MEANS GO

"Fear means go," says this hero.

"Fear is the space where you learn about yourself and prove to yourself that you can push through limitations. It's all about going for it, unleashing yourself. At the end of the day it's all about action."

That's Lara Galinsky, SVP of Echoing Green, whose mission is to unleash the next generation of talent to solve the world's biggest problems. Echoing Green provides seed funding for entrepreneurs who have big ideas to solve issues such as human rights abuses, hunger and poverty.

One example of their work has been helping Andrew Youn, co-founder of One Acre Fund, whose goal is to completely rethink how to solve the chronic hunger problem in Africa. Instead of food aid, which is at best a temporary solution, One Acre Fund has helped to radically improve local farm production through farm education, self-help groups, providing seeds and fertilizer, improving storage facilities and providing crop insurance. One Acre has grown from helping 30 farmers in 2006 to over 100,000 today.

Galinsky says fear is always part of change, whether it is entrepreneurs who may have concerns about their own limitations or the trepidations of all farmers across the African continent who have to unlearn thousands of years of doing things a certain way.

The bigger the change, the bigger the fear. Fear is one of the three core ideas Galinsky addresses in her recent book, *Work on Purpose.*

"Fear is the temperature gauge that you can use to tell if you have a fever," she says, "and that you need to look into the symptoms to see where it is coming from. And you need to not walk away from it, but go toward it. Because that's the kind of inflection point that allows you to really learn about yourself, and be able to prove to yourself what you can do — that you can do anything."

During all disruptions, good and bad, fear is our constant companion.

You must choose whether you will run toward it, or away from it. Chose whether fear will forge new possibilities within you, or new barriers in front of you.

There's All Different Kinds of Fear …
Every hero we interviewed embraced fear, in one way or another, so it could take them someplace new.

Fear of taking career or financial risks ...

"Life's scariest and most challenging moments are also moments of opportunity."

— Jessica Sager and Janna Wagner, co-founders of All Our Kin, a Connecticut-based nonprofit that trains and supports community child care providers

Fear of business failure or marketplace risks ...

"Don't wait. As a management team in a developing market, we don't have the luxury of perfect marketplace intelligence. You need to hone your intuition about what will work and what won't, and increase speed of execution so you're getting feedback very quickly."

— Kenneth Ng, CEO, Asia Pacific, American Standard

Fear for one's life ...

"I lived through what's known as the Dirty War in Argentina. When people in business say 'Oh, you undertake so many crazy ventures,' I tend to say, 'Well, not as risky as going to high school when I was growing up.' Once I experienced a fascist dictatorship that would randomly kill people, including my classmates from high school, my perception of risk was never the same."

— Martín Varsavsky, Argentine entrepreneur, philanthropist and founder of Fon, the world's largest Wi-Fi network — crowdsourced by people like you. If you share a little bit of your WiFi at home, you get free roaming at Fon spots worldwide in return.

And Then There's the Absolute Joy of Conquering One's Fear ...

Umeed Mistry is an underwater photographer and scuba instructor from India who works in the Laccadive Sea off the southern tip of India and the Andaman Islands, west of Myanmar.

"You learn so much about people when you take them out of their natural environment and bring them underwater," says Mistry.

"One of my students could only see about four inches away from her face. She was certified blind, so she couldn't drive, operate machinery, or do anything that most of us take for granted. During her first dive, I kept pulling her closer to the reef, thinking she'd want to be very close to appreciate the colors and textures of the coral. But she kept pulling away from me, away from the reef."

When they surfaced Mistry asked her why she kept pulling away. She replied, "When I'm on land, I spend so much time and effort making sure that when I'm walking, I don't fall. I constantly fear that I'll fall. So much of my concentration is going into just standing upright. When I'm in the water, it's such an incredible sense of freedom, all I want to do is be in deep water and swim around."

The sea released her from the daily fears and effort of just getting around.

During their next dive, Mistry took her away from the reef, into deeper waters. "She did somersaults. I watched this person go absolutely berserk with a sense of freedom! Because she didn't worry about the gravity-bound need to stay upright."

Many of those we interviewed said that's what it takes and that's what you get: Take yourself to a different place mentally, change what you do physically, and freedom can replace fear.

Unleash yourself.

Give yourself permission to anticipate and experience the joy on the other side of whatever you fear.

And do not hesitate.
In a disruptive world, there's always somebody behind you who has already unleashed their fear.
Hesitate and you'll get run over by someone who is pursuing their joy.

Getting Started

If fear still means *stop* to you, here are a few suggestions from our heroes:

- Surround yourself with those who already know that fear means *go*.

  Let great teammates, leaders and mentors show you the way.

- Do one thing each day that scares you.

  Start small. With fears that can be tackled in a day. You only truly feel brave once you've completed something. Those baby steps add up to courage!

- Confidence is a muscle.
  Exercise it constantly.

  Shape your will, and your body and to-do list will follow.

Never Hesitate: Key Takeaways ...

- Fear means *go*.
  It is the space where you can
  unleash yourself, and accomplish
  most anything.

- Do not hesitate.
  In a disruptive world, that will
  get you run over by the person
  behind you who has already
  pushed past their fears.

For More: Click, The Journey Continues, page 202
  - Fear: Acknowledge It, But Keep Disrupting Anyway

HABIT 17
NEVER ACCEPT DINGLESS TOOLS

YOU CAN'T PUT A DING IN THE UNIVERSE WHEN YOUR TOOLS SUCK

"We now have a novel and unprecedented and powerful set of technologies for deeply empowering people, for treating them like they're the most important part of the company, as opposed to cogs in some machine that just executes business processes," says this hero.

"We have this amazing toolkit now to do what Nelson Mandela described as the work of the leader: To find everyone's spark of genius in the organization.

"We have never had better tools to let people manifest what their particular spark of genius is, and it's time to get out of the way.

"Deploy the tools that let people come together, interact, collaborate, share, harvest the good things that emerge. And lead from behind and lead by example."

That's Andrew McAfee, principle research scientist at the Center for Digital Business at the MIT Sloan School of Management. He's also author of *Enterprise 2.0* and *Race Against the Machine*, both about how workers and leaders are being left behind by advances in technology.

McAfee continued, "Managers need to be comfortable with giving up control. … They need to give up these notions about how rigid control and brilliant process design are always the right answer. And get out of the way."

It is altogether fitting that McAfee, along with musician-activist Bono and others, spoke at the TED 2013 conference in a session called Progress Enigma. He and many of today's top management observers are calling attention to a crippling paradox inside most institutions.

Too many companies still build their technology infrastructures in ways that weigh down, instead of fully freeing, all the human potential inside those companies. Yes, the advances we've made in the past couple of decades in efficiencies and innovation are truly amazing! They are due in large part to our use of enabling technologies. But the advances are nowhere near as great or amazing as our potential.

Simply said, many corporate infrastructures still suck.

Great news:
We are in the midst of a major revolution in how we get stuff done, in how we do great work.

Lousy news:
Business seems to be waging war with its workforce. Work 2.0 advancements are being greatly hampered and slowed to a crawl.

(See Legoues' joke, page 63, about corporate security people wishing they could lock up all our cell phones.)

No Joke:
About Three Quarters of Us Are Still Working With Weights Tied Around Our Ankles

With a smartphone or tablet, you have unlimited capability to access anything or anyone. Awesome!

Yet, for many of us, instead of soaring, that freedom and power slows to a crawl once we have to integrate our own technologies with the systems that our employers have built for us to use.

In 2012, the Jensen Group completed its research on *Work 2.0: Ten Year Report*, a study of how companies have fared in the shift from Work 1.0, where the emphasis was on *organizational* productivity, to Work 2.0, which is about far greater *personal* productivity. While technology is already racing past 2.0 levels, many employers have yet to make the necessary shifts on issues of power, control, risk and trust in order to leverage today's technological capabilities.

Among the *Work 2.0: Ten Year Report* findings:

- About 30% of us are still stuck in Work 1.0 environments
- About 50% of us work in the weeds — a very confusing mess of 1.0 rules and tools and 2.0 tools

(Those two percentages combined mean that at least three quarters of us are being pulled down —our output is greatly hampered.)

- About 20% of us are in pure Work 2.0 (and beyond) environments

- Only 12% of us respond favorably that our employers respect our time as an asset to be invested. (Almost 9 in 10 of us believe that companies waste a lot of our time in order to boost organizational productivity.)

- Only 33% of us believe that our corporate tools and infrastructure are as good as they need to be. (That score drops significantly— a lot worse — when people compare what their corporate tools can do to what their own smartphones can do.)

Most of us have access to the greatest empowering technologies in the history of humanity.

At the same time, most infrastructures built by our employers are still corporate-centered — designed to deliver company success, but not necessarily yours.

This is holding many of us back.

The challenge is not technological.

What is required to move all of us into Work 2.0 — and beyond — are serious changes in how power, control, risk and trust are handled.

Never Accept Dingless Tools

This chapter's title is inspired by Steve Jobs who famously said that he wanted to create things that would put a ding in the universe — fulfilling his vision that design and technology can change the world.

In a world that's being disrupted by everybody else, and requires the same of you, you cannot afford to have anything less than tools and a corporate infrastructure that live up to that kind of vision — that empower you to be the best you can be. Kick-ass, personal-tool-based corporate infrastructures.

Yet here is today's reality: Around three quarters of us are stuck with an unhealthy mess, where personal productivity needs are constantly overridden by organizational productivity priorities.

So what can you do if that statistic feels like your current situation?

There Are Three Ways Out of This …
1. Be Good Enough to Be Lucky and Blessed …

About 20 percent of today's employers have already leapt into Work 2.0 and beyond. If you need to be somebody else's employee, hopefully you're lucky enough to work for one of these companies. Examples of these types of firms are most every company mentioned in this book, or those currently among *Fortune's* best places to work, or among *Fast Company's* or *Forbes'* most innovative firms.

Eventually, 20 percent will grow into 100 percent. Every company will have to build Work 2.0 infrastructures that focus as much on your personal productivity as they do on organizational productivity. However, if you're not currently employed at one of those companies and can't afford to wait for *eventually* — then you might want to try 2 or 3 ("Start a Business" or "Do Workarounds," see below).

2. Start a Business ...

Have an affair on your boss (Habit 12). Start your own firm. That way, your smartphone is the company's main tool, and the cloud is your infrastructure.

3. Do Workarounds ...

The core idea behind most every disruptive technology is that it allows the user to work around the way things are currently done, bypassing personal barriers. Examples from our heroes:

Ben Berkowitz is co-founder of SeeClickFix, which ties crowdsourced observations of downed power lines or potholes or neighborhood problems into the databases and project schedules of the government agencies that fix them. This simple app works around a lot of the bureaucracy that all citizens used to have to endure.

Michael Karnjanaprakorn is co-founder of Skillshare, which is democratizing education, where we all teach each other. This simple idea has spawned many new work-arounds, such as MOOCs, Massive Open Online Courses, where anyone who joins helps grade other students' work and helps to coach fellow students as well.

Chris Naegelin is co-founder of Spotflux, which is devoted to protecting your digital privacy and can encrypt all your Internet traffic. During his interview, Naegelin shared how doctors documenting cancer treatments in China used Spotflux to work around that country's firewall and post what they found on the Internet.

If you would like to apply these ideas — bypassing bureaucracy, democratizing training and development, working around your company's too-restrictive firewall — to completely reinvent how you get your work done, you don't have to wait for your leadership team to sanction it.

Sites like Lifehacker, Fried Beef's Tech, Dumb Little Man and others — or Googling "how to hack" or "how to work around" — will provide you all the step-by-step instructions you need.

If You Are a Corporate Leader:
Start building infrastructures that are a lot more user-centered. You may cringe at what that will do to your views on controls and risk-management — but it's actually enlightened self-interest.

If You Are an Employee:
Refuse to be burdened.

- Work for an employer who gets it.

- Or … have affairs on your boss, so that your smartphone is your corporate infrastructure.

- Or … work around what's holding you back.

The Geek Shall Inherent the Earth
Closing advice from SeeClickFix's Berkowitz: "Everyone should learn how to code. If you want to do innovation well, you may need to be your own technical co-founder."

Mitch Resnick, who directs the Lifelong Kindergarten group at MIT's Media Lab, echoed this thought in a TEDx talk on teaching kids to code: "Young people today are learning to code, but more importantly, they're coding to learn. [It's like] when you learn to read and write, it opens up opportunities for you to learn so many other things."

With services like Yapp and Scratch, and sites like appmakr, even code virgins can create amazing tools on their own.

Both Berkowitz's and Resnick's points should not be ignored: Get geeky or lose control of your future.

Never Hesitate: Key Takeaways ...

- Never accept any infrastructure or work tools that don't put a ding in the universe.

  In a disruptive world — where enabling technologies are so crucial — sucky tools will greatly hamper your ability to be your best.

For More: Click, The Journey Continues, page 202
- Measuring How Good or Bad Your Company's Tools Are

HABIT 18
DON'T KNOCK DOWN, BUILD ANEW

KINDNESS, OPTIMISM AND CARING TRUMP BRUTE FORCE

"Many would 'little lady' me. But I kept talking to people until I found those who would help me. If they couldn't help me directly, I wouldn't get off the phone until they gave me some names.

"The most important thing was to be kind and to think of others. Kill them with kindness," says this hero.

"It makes you stand out. It makes people remember you. It makes people more willing to accept your ideas and your thoughts. And when you're upset about something that needs to be fixed, it makes them take you more seriously because you're usually pretty jovial.

"From the janitor to the CEO, treat them with kindness. It's amazing how much easier everybody's lives would be if they took this approach."

That's Cinda Boomershine, owner of cinda b USA, one of the fastest-growing handbag, tote and accessories firms in the country. To achieve that, Boomershine had to persevere on two fronts: dealing with the male-dominated ol'boy fabric industry, and fighting to stay USA-made. Both were uphill battles — one economically, the other by disrupting the standard back-slapping ways of doing deals.

Her kindness towards others begins with her outlook on life. "I'm an eternal optimist," says Boomershine. That means that I always assume that good things will happen and that I have to push to find that positive solution."

She concludes: "I also believe that every challenge is also an opportunity. Usually when there are roadblocks or obstacles or things go wrong — which happens all the time in manufacturing — you end up with a better result, just because you had to jump through those hoops."

More Than Just the Golden Rule

It is crucial to understand what's behind this call for optimism and caring. Although it is a call for kindness to all — Yahoo CEO Marissa Mayer told us "I only deal with nice people" — it's not *just* that.

Most often, your biggest challenges will be people issues.

That's because every disruption asks someone to change the way they think, what they believe, what they do.

So killing them with kindness includes:
Igniting their imaginations …
Exciting their hearts, minds and passions …
Providing comfort or security …
Spreading joy …

John Danner gets this. He is one of the disruptive heroes changing the face of education. He was co-founder of Rocketship Education, whose mission to eliminate the achievement gap between low-income elementary students and all other elementary school students. Rocketship's seven schools are among the top-performing low-income schools in California, and they have plans to take their charter school model national.

Rocketeers (students) are achieving high levels of performance with a mix of high-tech and high-touch — individualized learning through its computer-based Learning Labs, supported by lots of one-on-one tutoring, coaching and instruction. The model supports Danner's personal goal of shaking things up, "Disrupt by doing something that works more effectively and using it competitively against the existing system."

Does that fill traditional school systems and administrators with joy, and leave them feeling comfortable and secure? Obviously not. "You don't want to adapt," Danner challenges the traditionalists, "that's OK. Rocketship will just keep serving more and more children." The imaginations that Danner is looking to fire up are those of grade schoolers like Santiago, and his mom.

"When we first started working with Santiago, he was a third grader," says Danner. "His cume file [the permanent record of a student] was two inches thick with all sorts of reports about him being a problem child and that he'd never amount to anything. We found the problem very quickly. Santiago was actually very smart — a standard deviation or two above the norm. He was sitting in classrooms that catered to the lowest-performing students and he got in lots of trouble because he was always bored.

"Within a year of going to Rocketship, he went from being steered to special schools for problem kids to being advanced in both English/language arts and math. What was also amazing was his mother ending up working at Rocketship, and then going back to college.

"In our business, you do what you do for reasons of the heart. Santiago's story represents that," Danner concludes.

Disruptive change will always upset somebody — because you're messing with their status quo.

In a disruptive era, the best way to be kind and caring to everyone is to build anew — create wonderful new worlds and invite everyone to join you.

Some will refuse to go. That's OK. Move on … with no regrets.

At the end of the day, the passions and imaginations you need to fire up are those who will join you.

If you examine the common themes among the 100 heroes, you will find deeply caring and kind people — the same people who are perfectly OK if those who are pissed off need to be left behind.

Jamie Heywood of PatientsLikeMe cares deeply about all patients who need help, and he doesn't care what the FDA or Big Pharma thinks about what he's doing.

Caterina Fake, who — through Creative Commons, Etsy, Hunch, Flickr and more — is upsetting a lot of people who like business as usual, speaks as lovingly about employees, partners and customers as she does about her own daughter.

Vishen Lakhiani of Mindvalley wants to build the world's best place to work and rethink his country's brain drain, yet he's doing so in ways that would strike fear in the hearts of most HR managers, who know they can't deliver anything similar.

It was Lakhiani who channeled this quote: "You never change things by fighting the existing reality. To change something, build a new model that makes the existing model obsolete." — Buckminster Fuller

Don't knock down. Build anew.
It's an amazing way to show that you care.

Getting Started ...

1. Be a good person,
   just like Mom taught you to be.
   Spend your life on things that will outlast your life.

   Do good work. Raise good kids. Consider others.
   Be nice.

2. Do epic shit.
   See Habit 4.

Don't Knock Down, Build Anew: Key Takeaways ...

- In a disruptive world — most often, your biggest challenges will be people issues.

- Always kill people with kindness. But do so in a way that also ignites their hearts and minds.

  Build wonderful new worlds and invite everyone to join you. Care for everyone by building a new and amazing future.

For More: Click, The Journey Continues, page 202
- Care ... and Also Move On

Guiding Principles

LIVE THESE

7 HABITS FOR SAVING THE WORLD,
HAVING A GREAT LIFE

"Those are my principles
and if you don't like them …
well, I have others."

~ Groucho Marx

PREAMBLE
DISRUPTIVE GUIDING PRINCIPLES

What makes you … you?

Your answer will determine a lot of what you do with these 25 habits.

Every interview with every hero began with that question. A pattern began to emerge before we were even half way into our search for all 100 heroes.

> The willingness to explore and then deeply know thyself (Habit 19)
> and the courage to follow your passions and convictions (Habit 20)
> are the core around which everything revolves.

This is especially true in a disruptive world.

Want to kick butt and do amazing things while everything around you is blowing up? Then know thyself deeply.

Want to benefit from or take advantage of continuous disarray, disorder and disruption? Then have the courage to do what fires your soul and take principled stands. (And the wisdom to know when to hold back on that!)

Most important …

If your first thought is, "How do I do that?"

… you're barking up the wrong tree.

How is the wrong question.

(See Coda: Everything Is Figureoutable)

Asking *how* too quickly reduces everything to a checklist of to-dos without the required fire in your belly that makes everything work.

Instead …

Seek what lies within each hero's story.

They didn't jump to *how* questions.

They asked and answered questions like …

- Why?
  — Why do it this way?
  — Why not do it differently?
  — Why not change it?

- What would I do if I knew I could not fail?

- What legacy do I want to leave?

- What do I care about that's far bigger than me?
- What *really* matters?
  In this situation, and always?
- What is the crossroad at which I find myself at this point?
- What commitment am I willing to make?
- What fears do I need to face and push past?
- What course of action would set me free?
- What are my ahas?
  Am I going to act on them?
- Am I willing to hold myself accountable for the change I want to see?
- What can I do that would make the most difference for the most people?

Those who thrive in a disruptive world ask and answer questions like these before they ever think about *how* questions.

They take for granted that how will be figureoutable as they go.

They also know that in a disruptive world whatever they choose to work on could **completely change the answer to all *how* questions. That's the point of disruption!**

Some of the questions here were based on Peter Block's *The Answer to How is Yes* as well as Simon Sinek's *Start With Why*.

HABIT 19 ✓
KNOW THYSELF, DEEPLY

THE BEDROCK THAT HOLDS EVERYTHING TOGETHER

"I started to panic on my way to my first interview to become a university professor. I realized that this wasn't the choice that would make me happy," says this hero.

"I realized that I shouldn't do something just because I'm good at it. That's actually a poor reason to do something. I decided I should be doing things because they make me happy or because they make me a better person or a more fulfilled person.

"While I was taking some time to think about what to do, my brother told me about some local poker games. I loved it! I think I became successful because I was willing to spend 12 hours a day learning the game, and I wasn't willing to do that to be a professor."

That's Annie Duke, also known as The Duchess of Poker. Duke is widely recognized as one of the best female poker players in the world. In 2004, she won the inaugural World Series of Poker (WSOP) prize of $2,000,000. She has tutored actor Ben Affleck, taught at the WSOP Academy, and jokingly calls herself a media whore for all her television appearances. Not all her bets have turned out to be winners, though. She was co-founder of the Epic Poker League which filed for bankruptcy in 2012 after only one year amidst controversy over how she ran the organization.

Failures and all, she wouldn't have it any other way: "I grew up in a family where you were kind of forced into choices. You could either decide that you wanted to conform, or you could decide that eccentricity and being different and pushing boundaries was what you would value.

"What I realized about happiness for me is that it's doing things because they inspire you and make you feel fulfilled, and not to worry about the other stuff. I never wanted to be one of those people who woke up at 60 not having lived the life I wanted to live," she concludes.

Pre-Work for Everything

Most heroes said that key to both being disruptive and dealing with disruptions was following one's passion (Habit 20). And then they hastened to add that you can't do that unless you truly understand who you are.

> The universal pre-work for a disruptive era: know thyself, deeply.

Surprisingly, many of us think we know ourselves, but do not.

"I sometimes think we should have named our course *Waterboarding for MBAs*," jokes Cheryl Kiser, Executive Director of Babson College's Social Innovation Lab. "With many business students, no one has ever asked them 'What matters to you?' They're learning all about what matters to shareholders and customers and markets, but none of that is useful unless they know what matters to them. They really need to know themselves better."

Most successful senior execs have done this pre-work and readily acknowledge that it's part of what made them successful.

"My parents are an influence in my life all the time," shares Marissa Mayer, CEO of Yahoo. "My father was an engineer, my mother was an art teacher. In what I do — which is a blend of engineering and art and product management and other pieces — you can feel both of their passions and what they gave me in terms of appreciation for the world."

Mayer continues, "Even though I've lived in California now longer than I did in Wisconsin, where I grew up, I still feel very Midwestern through and through. The work ethic and values system that comes from that is an important part of me."

Oxfam Great Britain CEO Mark Goldring also draws upon his childhood to fully understand what drives him: "I was part of an Army family, so we were dragged from Army base to Army base. There were big cultural differences most everywhere we went. We were never in one place for very long, so I had to build lots of little lives. Which gave me a sense of restlessness. So today I feel I've got to make the best of what I've got now in the moment. … I can't say this is what it's going to be like forever. … Let's just get on with the present."

Not surprisingly, Goldring's advice is the same as what we heard from so many heroes: "First and foremost, you must really understand yourself. Because few of us ever change who we really are. So think very hard about who you are — reflecting on your own achievements, your own failures, your own experiences — to get a real understanding of who you are and in what direction you need to go and how far you can push that. Because you can push it … we all do. But we have to push ourselves in a way that's true to who we originally are."

In a postscript to those thoughts, when we interviewed Goldring he was CEO of Mencap, a firm helping those with learning disabilities. He later emailed to say that when the Oxfam GB opportunity presented itself, the interviewers asked him follow-up questions based on his *Disruptive Heroes* video. "So there you go!" he says after being offered the new position — knowing thyself and putting it out there really does make a difference. "I wasn't ready to leave [his old position], but this is my lifelong dream job."

Always Important:
Even More So in a Disruptive World

More and more, you are going to be called upon to make major decisions, with almost no information — or worse, totally conflicting information — and very little to draw upon but your understanding of yourself and what truly matters. So knowing thyself must be the foundation for all major and quick decisions.

"One should make a decision quickly when it's time to make a decision," says this hero.

"When my wife told me of her dream, within a minute or so I had made up my mind. 'Yes … why not?'

"Make a quick decision and then one should stick to it. If one is clear in one's mind, and one is sincere in the cause and shares it with others, there are many good people who will come to assist and support."

That's Mumtaz Ali, founder and managing trustee of UM Healthcare, which he launched to care for the needy in rural Pakistan in response to his late wife's request as she died of cancer. UM Healthcare treats over 35,000 patients annually, 90 percent of whom live below the poverty line. To aid their local staff, UM Trust developed a global tele-healthcare system, in collaboration with Stanford University, USAID and others, where doctors from around the world assist in diagnosing their patients.

Ali shared that his wife, in the final weeks of her illness, said that she'd had a dream where she was told to establish a healthcare facility in their rural village. Within minutes, Ali agreed to dedicate their small plot of land and life savings to this project.

Decisions like that — disrupting one's life and quickly taking advantage of global disruptions in healthcare systems — require a solid foundation of knowing oneself and one's values.

In a disruptive world, ordinary everyday decisions require the same foundation.

More and more, difficult decisions need to be made very quickly. To make good decisions, you need inner clarity.

That kind of clarity comes only from truly knowing oneself.

Getting Started:

You are already on a lifelong journey to truly know yourself. Here is a journaling exercise to simply clarify and leverage what you already know ...

- Answer in one to three pages:
  What makes you ... you?

    Every interview with every hero began with this question. A few stumbled through it, but most could quickly reel off one, two or three stories about moments in their lives that forged who they are.

    They were able to quickly articulate what makes them who they are, and how they leverage that in their everyday activities. We all need that kind of clarity. Restricting your entire life to just a couple of pages helps to create the inner clarity you need.

Know Thyself, Deeply: Key Takeaways ...

- Pre-work for doing anything in a disruptive era:
  Know thyself, deeply.

- Develop your Inner Voice
  to make better decisions, faster.

For More: Click, The Journey Continues, page 202
  - Five Ways To Confirm or Change Your Inward Journey

HABIT 20 ✓
OF COURSE ...
FOLLOW YOUR PASSION

DO WHAT FIRES YOUR SOUL

"At some point, we're all going to die. And you want to make sure your life on this planet was worthwhile and you have no regrets.

"I've spent a lot of time in nursing homes talking to old people. You can learn a lot from people as they're ending their lives. Three regrets came up continuously. They wished that they learned more: that they got more education. They wished that they fell in love with the right person: marrying who they really loved. Lastly, they wished that they had followed their dreams.

"When you're about to die, are you going to leave happy about these three things?" asks this hero.

"I see myself living a life with no regrets. So, seize the moment. When presented with two paths, pick the one that will make you happy."

That's Yao Huang, Founder of The Hatchery which helps startup companies and entrepreneurs refine their business models and pitches and then connects them with potential investors. She is also CEO of Gigapixel Creative, a web design and marketing agency. *Forbes* named Huang one of the 11 women at the center of New York's digital scene, and she traveled with Secretary of State Hillary Clinton to Indonesia in 2011 as a member of the Global Entrepreneurship Program.

"I am probably a lot like many of you who are watching this," Huang says in her interview video. "I started working in Fortune 500 companies, had good jobs, was paid good money. And then I started feeling antsy and decided to jump ship to follow my passions. What made that happen was my knowing that even if I completely fail and fall flat on my face, I can go back and get a job. Once I figured that out, everything became easy."

Huang continues: "There are two things behind following your passion: breaking through fear and creating freedom. I created my own freedom by leaving my career and going out on my own and building companies with some friends. That led to something inside me: It's all mental. Each of us need to create freedoms within ourselves, in what we believe.

"On the fear issue, I was always the shyest person in the back of the room. As I tried to break through barriers — fear of heights, jumping out of a plane; fear of public speaking, just getting up there and doing it — I realized just trying gave me the confidence to try even more. Trying creates confidence."

Huang's closing advice: "Just jump. Don't think, just do."

In a disruptive world, if you are
not following your passion,
everyone else's disruptions
will push you into following theirs.

Pick the path that makes you happy.

Create your own freedoms —
beginning with your state of mind.

The Natural Next Step
That Follows Know Thyself, Deeply

Once you truly know who you are, what you stand for, why you're on this planet … following your dreams or passions is the inevitable next step.

"In 2009, I made a journey from Kampala, Uganda, where I worked as an accountant, to visit my mother in the village where I was born," shares this hero.

"On my way there, I met my kid sister carrying a huge bundle of firewood on her head. When she saw me, she started to cry so hard that I was scared. Was our mother dead?

'No,' she said. She had missed school that day just to gather wood for the family.

"That day, I decided to do something about this."

That's Sanga Moses, who launched Eco-Fuel Africa, which turns farm and municipal waste into clean-burning fuel briquettes. Not just to save kids like his sister from having to lose school days to gather wood. But also to have an impact on deforestation in Africa — every year Africa loses forests equal to the size of Switzerland.

From that passionate wake-up call, Moses also built a financial eco-system to help address Africa's health problems. Cooking over wood fires is mostly done indoors, resulting in about two million deaths per year from diseases and health problems from breathing in all that smoke. Moses created a network of women retailers who are trained to help their communities change their cooking practices. These women, who previously had no way to make any money, now earn five dollars per day as retailers for the briquettes.

Every disruptive dream, career and business is different. Yet they all share a common bond with Sanga Moses — they began with that person's internal passions.

"Diversity has always been a part of me, an integral part of who I am. The way I view my life, the way I work, the way I do my job on a day-to-day basis," said Tony Tenicela.

Tenicela has been an entrepreneur, worked on the team that developed Travelocity, and has been with IBM for 16 years, currently as Global Leader and Business Development Executive. As an openly gay IBM senior exec, he advises corporations how to leverage diversity and human capital as well as LGBT policies as strategic business drivers. His passion is helping leaders — especially in China — develop strong and vibrant business cases for diversity in the workplace.

Tenicela's views on diversity were formed as a child traveling the world with his father. "As a physician, my father was invited to different countries to set up clinics. I was exposed to so many different foods and cultures and people — his staff was multicultural from many different countries. As a result, I have always looked at life through a multifaceted lens."

Beyond the usual ways of defining diversity, Tenicela says "There's now more attention being placed on diversity of thought. This is about the ability to understand and appreciate everyone's ideas and experiences." This area is his current passion.

"So many people think that conformity is the standard. That you can't break away from conformity," he concludes. "They don't realize that if all of us were comfortable with being ourselves and thinking out of the box on a daily basis, the amount of innovation would be amazing!"

The more comfortable you are with yourself, the more you follow your passions.

The more people follow their passions, the greater the increase in innovations.

It's that simple.
And that important.

Follow Your Passion: This Advice Was Universal:
"Follow your own path."

— Jamie Heywood, co-founder, PatientsLikeMe

"We're only here for a split second of time in the grand scheme of things. We won't get a second chance. Follow your dreams. Go do whatever feels right and you can be proud of."

> — Ken Banks, founder, kiwanja.net, which works throughout Africa to help entrepreneurs use mobile-phone technology to drive local innovations

"A great manager — a truly great manager — will transform work based on an understanding of what is important to each individual: What is it that they throw themselves into with great passion? Transform their work to match that."

> — Caterina Fake, co-founder, Hunch and Flickr

"Most of us invest in a future that will come years from now. That's why we go to college. You also need to ground yourself in today — do things today that you were waiting to do next year. Push your boss a little bit harder and say I want to do this now. A lot of people don't get what they want because they don't ask. A lot of what I've received in life was because I had the audacity to ask for it and pursue it."

> — Manick Bhan, founder, Rukkus

Getting Started:

A journaling exercise:

- Write a one-to-three page Legacy Letter to a loved one: Part of your legacy is sharing why that loved one must follow *their* dreams.

  As humans, we have an unbelievable ability to bullshit ourselves: "Oh, I can't pursue my passion because …"

When writing a letter to a loved one — spouse, son or daughter, closest friend — advising them to follow their dreams, suddenly all that bullshit fades away. Give a copy to them, keep a copy for yourself.

On your copy, cross out their name, insert yours.

Guaranteed: You will instantly know what you need to do.

Of Course... Follow Your Passion: Key Takeaways ...

- In a disruptive world,
  following your passion is an important part of seizing control of your future.

  If you don't, you will be forever pursuing the other guy's disruptive passion.

- At some point, you are going to die.
  Make sure you die happy,
  with no regrets.

For More: Click, The Journey Continues, page 202
- Writing a Legacy Letter: Detailed Instructions

HABIT 21
RESILIENCE MATTERS

"I like to blow shit up," says Cindy Gallop. In many ways, it's her world and we're just renting space in it!

Cindy Gallop has been disrupting things her whole life. When asked what makes her that way, she replies simply, "à la Lady Gaga, I was born this way."

Her CV says that she's an advertising consultant, founder and former chair of the U.S. branch of advertising firm Bartle Bogle Hegarty. She went viral in 2009 with a TED talk about her sexplorations and the accompanying website, MakeLoveNotPorn.com, where she is redefining porn for the 21st century. And her 2013 talk at the SXSW conference on this topic was also a show-stopper!

Yet her efforts in crowdsourcing how we get stuff done may have an even bigger and longer lasting impact. IfWeRanTheWorld.com focuses on breaking all work into micro-actions. "The single biggest untapped resource in the world is human good intentions that never get translated into actions," she says. "Micro-actions are simply taking the first step in whatever you want to accomplish and then turning it over to the world to finish the next steps."

Gallop's idea is to get people share their If I Ran The World ideas — an example on the site is making the world a more bicycle-friendly place — and then take any of the no-big-deal mini-steps that others have laid out. Micro-actions can end up having a pretty big impact.

Jeans-maker Levi's worked with IfWeRanTheWorld to create a campaign to revitalize the manufacturing town of Braddock, Pennsylvania.

This one idea of micro-actions may completely reinvent how we think about our role in work. Or it may not. It may be yet another disruptive flash in the pan.

That doesn't matter.

Regardless of which disruptive ideas take off and which ones will fizzle out, the one thing to remember is that they will not stop coming. That's why the Cindy Gallops and Garrett Camps and Dominic Murens of the world run so much of ours.

This means that resilience is the foundational skillset and approach toward life in the 21st-century.

Resilience: The Next Big Thing

"The world is not as stable as you think it is. How are you preparing yourself to deal with that instability?" asks this hero.

"Going forward, the buzzword is going to be 'Resilience.' 'Sustainable' doesn't mean anything when the game keeps changing around you. Even if you're tuned perfectly, your supply chain could fall out next week, or China could have some horrible epidemic, or war could create instant raw material-interruptions.

"That means you have to design for overlaps in who is doing what and with changes in how things get done. What results may be slightly less efficient, but it's the answer for an unpredictable world."

That's Dominic Muren, founder of The Humblefactory, which designs frameworks and plans for open-source manufacturers, helping entrepreneurs around the world build the things that mainstream manufacturing won't or can't make for them.

Muren continues, "As part of designing differently, you need to find ways to leverage the people that you have or the people you interact with so that you enhance resilience. One of the ways we do that at The Humblefactory is open IP [intellectual property]. We believe that there's no reason to have closed IP. If you participate in an open community, you get more and better ideas because you have more people thinking about things. You have better access to more minds."

Completely open IP? Anyone who has created a product or brand will go crazy over that idea. Patents would be meaningless. Royalties and sales for artists would plummet to nothing. And yet, it's already here and being thrust into our lives by the Dominic Murens and Marcin Jakubowskis (see Habit 24) of the world.

The world is not as stable as you think it is. Everything you plan will be disrupted, continuously.

So: Don't resist that. Embrace it.

Resilience is the way forward:
Your ability to bounce back and keep heading in the same direction after being bent, folded, spindled, stretched and mutilated.

The Path to Resilience:
Continuous Learning and Unlearning.
Fast. Over and Over Again

This comes naturally to born-that-way disruptors like Cindy Gallop, Lady Gaga and Dominic Muren.

How do the rest of us — who may not have been born that way — learn how to learn and unlearn faster than we ever have before?

We searched for patterns and solutions among the heroes who focused on education and training and development. What emerged were not any big revelations about how to learn, but more about a disruptive philosophy of life — guiding principles that look a lot like the laws that preceded this one:

"The only problem is always, always, always having the will to do better. When I look at things I did even just a week before, I continually think, 'Oh my God, I was so stupid.' All of us have to be thinking that … one week from now, and the week after that, and the week after that, we have to keep saying, 'Oh my God, I was so stupid.' That's the will to do better."

— Marco De Rossi, Founder of OilProject,
an Italian-based online school where all classes are
free and all teachers are volunteers.

"You have to put your ass on the line, in everything you do. Why? Because it's the right thing to do. Take the baton and cross the finish line. Because societally, we're moving there. Take the leap. Also, to do that, you will need to build a circle of ambassadors who will join you. The social dimension of accountability is so important. Finally, you have to wake up every day and say 'How am I going to make a difference with your team and the organization?' Doing that every day will keep you learning every day."

— Dan Pontefract, author of *Flat Army*, senior director, Learning and Collaboration at Telus, the Canadian-based telecommunications firm.

"Think big.

"Set your goals and stick to them.

"Be creative in how you achieve those goals.

"Stick your neck out, doing whatever you think is the right thing to do.

"Be so good at what you're doing that it doesn't matter if you get fired. If things go wrong, other companies or other project will pick up where getting fired left off.

"Package things in an absolutely superior way. Go out of your way to make a compelling case and to convince others that your way is the right way. If they still say no, just do it.

"Start small, pilot it and prove your ideas and go from there."

— Stefaan van Hooydonk is Head of Philips Lighting University at Philips Lighting

The key to resilience is continuous learning and unlearning … fast!

Key to that is:

- Get shit done, fast
- Be accountable for everything
- Skin your knees …
  when things don't go exactly as planned…
- Explore why
- Learn
- Grow
- Move on

Repeat that cycle above for the rest of your life.

Getting Started:

See above. 'Nuf said.

Resilience Matters: Key Takeaways …

- Everything you plan or do will be disrupted, continuously.

- So the only path forward is to to become more and more resilient.

- Success is how quickly you learn and bounce back after being bent, folded, spindled, stretched and mutilated.

For More: Click, The Journey Continues, page 202
- Building Resiliency Through Micro-Actions

HABIT 22 ✓
DISRUPT YOURSELF

"I was talking with my brother, who was doing his MBA at MIT in Boston. I told him I'm desperate: I'm sitting in Spain with two babies, and I had this crazy idea of using viruses to work with drugs.

I have this idea, but I don't know what to do.

"He said, 'Ask Mom to take care of the boys and you come here.'

"So I did. And then I saw the light," she says, laughing loudly as if a beam from above bonked her on the head. "I found people who believed in me and my ideas. What I found in Boston was just so appealing, I couldn't let it go."

That's Elisabet de los Pinos. And she is on a mission to eradicate cancer. Named by *Time* magazine as one of the ten entrepreneurs who will change your life, she founded Aura Biosciences to create nanodrugs — viruses that can attack cancer cells and only those cells.

"I tell people that future generations are going to judge me by our ability to cure cancer and that's what I'm here to do," she proudly proclaims. "I'm not here to improve life survival for one month. I'm here to cure it."

None of that would have been possible if she hadn't disrupted herself — moving her life, as well her two young boys, to a new country and in a completely new direction.

Like many of us, de los Pinos could have avoided the risks, trouble and pain of disrupting her family and career. "At first," she shared, "everyone thought I was crazy in taking on these life changes." Still, she just had to jump. She knew that her world — the race to cure cancer — would pass her by if she didn't jump.

Her view on what it takes to disrupt oneself: "You need to realize that you are strong, much stronger than you think." And once you take the leap, "You just need to plan for only six months, because whatever is going to happen, a lot will change during those first few months, and you will need to adapt."

And what if unanticipated challenges arise? De los Pinos shared, "What did my parents give me? Not money. They gave me this [both hands pointing to the top of her head] so that I can think. And if I can think, I'm sure I will get out of it."

Do Unto You Before Others Do It for You

Disrupting oneself is not just for people on save-the-world quests. It's applicable to everyone.

There is only one certainty in this uncertain world — at any moment, often when you are least prepared for it, you will be disrupted by forces outside of your control. The only way to get ahead of this, to be proactive instead of reactive, is to do it to yourself. To start pushing changes into your career and life, especially during the times when it feels most comfortable to keep things as they are.

While many of our heroes expressed this view, Whitney Johnson popularized it. She is a founding partner of Rose Park Advisors, a Clayton Christensen investment firm based on his views on disruption.

Johnson translated Christensen's ideas on industry-wide change into how to manage personal disruption in an HBR series titled *Disrupt Yourself*. "The most overlooked engine of growth is the individual," she said. "If you are really looking to move the world forward, begin by innovating on the inside, and disrupt yourself."

She believes that the research findings on disruptive business innovations — the odds of success are six times higher and the revenue opportunities are 20 times greater — also apply to each of us as individuals.

You will get disrupted.
No doubt. Guaranteed.
The choice you need to make:
Will you be the one who does it to you?
If so, then you get to choose the
direction the disruption will take you.

Restructuring Personal Risk

Gib Bulloch is executive director of Accenture Development Partnerships, which brings one of the world's largest consulting firm's resources and expertise to not-for-profit organizations such as Oxfam, CARE International and The World Bank.

He created that position by disrupting not only how Accenture approached not-for-profit consulting, but also his own career. He realized something was tugging at him during a sabbatical from the firm, working as a volunteer in Macedonia, after NATO intervened to force Slobodan Milošević to withdraw his forces from neighboring Kosovo.

"I kept thinking about how much more I could have gotten done," he shared, "if I had all the resources of Accenture and my team helping me. I started wondering if there was a way for us to change our business model to make ourselves more affordable. The challenge was how to go beyond the traditional consulting pro-bono philanthropic model of providing free services to address not-for-profit issues."

Bulloch's idea was to harness Accenture's top performers' needs for personal development, as well as many of their passions to give back to society. Each Accenture executive who joined this group would agree to give up half of his/her salary for six months. Clients would still pay for services, but at greatly reduced fees, freed from the focus on profit margins and overhead.

Accenture agreed to provide top-level executives for six-month cross-cultural, cross-sector developmental opportunities, and each individual would also have skin in the game.

Bulloch did an internal feasibility study and found that there was a correlation between high-achieving performers that Accenture wanted to make sure they retained, and those who were interested in the program. That's what convinced senior leaders to green-light this idea.

Bulloch concludes, "This was not risk-free. I had to put a substantial portion of my salary on the line to back up this idea. The person I had to sell this to said, 'I'm used to people coming in and complaining that they're not paid enough. And you're coming in asking for a pay-cut. You've got my attention.'"

Disruption is never risk-free.
Disrupting yourself doesn't make risk go away.

What it does is restructure the risk:
You get to define the risk and
how it will effect you should anything
go wrong. And how it will benefit you,
and others, if things go well.

If you hesitate to disrupt yourself,
you are subject to whatever risks the
marketplace throws at you.

Good luck with that approach.

"The real voyage of discovery consists not in seeking new landscapes but in having new eyes." — Marcel Proust

For many, the biggest challenge in disrupting themselves is not risk or courage or knowing what to do. It is the willingness to see their situation with new eyes. To see that it is far better to disrupt yourself as the architect of that change, rather than wait for disruption to be thrust upon you.

Getting Started:
Courtesy of Whitney Johnson's TEDx Talk on disrupting yourself ...

1. Assess where you are, compared to where you want to be.

   If your trajectory needs a turbo-boost, you're a prime candidate for disrupting yourself.

2. Iterate, iterate, iterate. See Habit 7.

3. Embrace your constraints.
   Accenture's cap on its pro-bono work was the constraint that forced Bulloch to rethink his and the firm's approach.

4. Be impatient.
   Impatient for small quick wins, but also confident that the odds of success will swing in your favor when you live disruptively.

5. Start today.
   Dare to disrupt your own status quo.

Disrupt Yourself: Key Takeaways ...

- Disrupt yourself before the world does it to you. That way, you get to choose where the disruption will take you.

- Do it right now, before you've lost that choice.

For More: Click, The Journey Continues, page 202
- Top Tips: If It Feels Scary, You're on the Right Track

HABIT 23
YOUR POWER IS IN YOUR NETWORK

DO EXTRAORDINARY THINGS — TOGETHER. UNLEASH THE POWER OF THE GIFT ECONOMY

"We're now in a Florentine moment where people are beginning to understand the power of networks and beginning to understand how the right introduction at the right time can make a huge difference — in the same way that the right thinking at the right moment can totally change what's going on," says this hero.

"The reason I can do this connecting so well is that people trust me. People trust me not to waste their time. People trust me to protect them."

If you are launching a project where you're searching for 100 great disruptive heroes, a great place to begin would be to reach out to this world class connector. As we did.

Sunny Bates heads Sunny Bates Associates (SBA) in New York City, and is a curator of ideas, talent and disruption.

SBA works with clients to evaluate and select different strategies, reposition their businesses, and assess and optimize resources. Behind all that are deep personal connections.

For a quarter-century, long before today's social media popularized friending, Bates built a network of leaders and thinkers that happens to fuel brain-trust events such as TED and the World Economic Forum in Davos.

Some of her secrets, which also apply to each of her connections: "You've got to be a good listener. When I meet with people and they're all broadcast, I'm like 'Ah, no thank you.' I spend time with people who energize me. I have to come away excited, with new ideas, new thoughts … that's who I want to spend time with. Whenever you're with those people, you know you're going to go to a place — either intellectually or emotionally or both — that is totally exciting and nurturing and feeds you and will keep you going for a long time. They're almost always people who are living in the now, and not judging. Just observing and listening and reading the situation and power structure and influences, and knowing where to take the conversation next."

Bates is one of the premier connectors in the world, yet when asked why she isn't making a gazillion dollars as a head-hunter for these services, she says. "I can't take a fee for connecting people. I get paid to do strategy and to bring people together to come up with new ways of doing business. But beyond that, it's the gift economy."

The gift economy.

One of the key drivers of this disruptive age is the amazing advances made in all social media. Yet, still, so few understand that it's never been about the latest technology or meme or viral video or eye candy. It has always been about people helping people. Giving. Benefiting others.

Your Own Florentine Moment

We're already deep into social's Florentine moment where the power of networking is finally being leveraged. We've heard that from people like Seth Godin (*Tribes*), Clay Shirky (*Here Comes Everybody*), James Surowiecki (*The Wisdom of Crowds*) and the foursome who wrote one of the Internet's first social screeds, *The Cluetrain Manifesto*. They all tell us that your strongest power to get anything done lies within your network.

They all want us to know that ...

Your network is one of your
most important creations.
It is the backbone of your life, work,
career, goals and dreams.
Your network is the space where
magic can happen.

But for that magic to happen in the midst of constant chaotic disruptions, you are going to have to combine the power of today's social media and apps with the classic advice you got from Mom...

You only get as good as you give.
For magic to happen, you will have to
listen ... listen deeply.
And give generously.

To unleash the power of your network,
you need to create value for others,
long before you ask for or need something
in return.

The Power of Your Network
Is Based on the Power of Paying It Forward

When asked why they do what they do, so many of our heroes mentioned that someone helped them along the way, and helping others was the right thing to do as they built their network.

In 1916, author Lily Hardy Hammond wrote, "You don't pay love back; you pay it forward." That catchphrase, *pay it forward*, not only has became a part of our popular culture — from Robert Heinlein's and Ray Bradbury's sci-fi futures, to an exchange between Spiderman and the Hulk, to a 2000 film of the same name — it has been hard-wired into the networks and actions of today's disruptive heroes.

Debbie Berebichez shared one example of this. She is the first Mexican woman to complete a Ph.D. in physics from Stanford University. She went on to conduct further research at Columbia University, and currently works on Wall Street as a quant — one of those geeks who helps investors figure out when and where to invest.

Her disruptive side comes through when she talks about science. "I want to be known as the Oprah of science," she says. Her goal is to mix science and entertainment in such a way that today's youth see the abstractions of math and physics in exciting new ways that have meaning in their everyday lives. Everywhere she goes, she is building a network to accomplish this goal.

Her pay-it-forward moment came years before, before switching to science as a career. At Brandeis University, a teaching assistant, Rupesh, noticed her passion for physics, even though she was majoring in philosophy. She told him "I don't want to die without doing physics." Based on her passion, Rupesh tutored her 11 hours a day for three months straight so she could switch into physics. He refused to accept any pay.

"That is how my mission in life began," recalls Berebichez. After she successfully switched into physics, she asked Rupesh why he did all that work for her.

"He said to me, 'Debbie, I grew up in India, in Darjeeling, way up in the mountains. There was an old man who used to climb up the mountain every day to teach my sister and me music, English and math. And every time my father tried to compensate this old man, he refused to take any pay. He said, 'The only way you could repay me is if you do this for someone else in the world.'"

> Understand that while technological advances mean that we can friend everyone in the universe, the true power in your network comes from paying forward to others that which has been done for you.

The Power of Your Network
Is Your Ability to Constantly Create New Teams

Teams make work ... work. And your network is what determines your ability to constantly build new teams based on the demands of the moment.

There is perhaps no better example of this than the making of a movie. Hundreds, sometimes thousands, of people, most of whom have never worked together before, come together for a few months, passionately dedicate their lives to something they believe in and then disband. And what determined who got invited to join the project, and who accepted, was the power of the director's, actors' and producers' networks.

No one knows this better than Jon Landau. With James Cameron, he has produced two of the highest-grossing movies of all time, *Titanic* and *Avatar*, and is currently working on the next two Avatar movies, as well as *Battle Angel*, a film about a 26th-century female cyborg.

Says Landau, speaking first about being disruptive: "Jim wrote the first version of *Avatar* in 1996, before *Titanic* was released. But, at the time, the technology did not exist to tell the story the way it needed to be told — the ability to create a blue, nine-foot character, and have him be emotive and engaging in close-ups. By 2005, I said to Jim that it's time and that we could be an impetus for change with this movie.

"By the time it was released, we did change the rules. Prior to *Avatar*, there was a belief that our imaginations were limited by what was or was not possible. *Avatar* opened a crack in the door that demonstrated that anything is possible. If you can imagine it, there are people around you who can realize it."

Then Landau identified what made all that magic possible:

"Human capital is a huge focus for us. Jim and I are standing on the shoulders of others, and we can only stand as high as they build us up," Landau shares. "The team we pull together is critical to us. That's why the bonds you establish on a film are so strong."

As Landau says, each and every movie is a new startup business; the script is their business plan; and the talent is where and how the magic happens.

In a disruptive world, you will constantly
rotate onto and off teams.

You are only as good as your ability
to form, or get picked for, your next team.
The depth of your network —
how deep each of your connections is —
is one of the biggest drivers in each
of those team selections.

Getting Started:

1. Become a power-user of social media.
   Participate fully in the current
   shift in power.

   You must be using key online networks.

   But **not because** you should be improving your
   Klout score, or launching the next meme, or amass-
   ing an army of online friends.

   As Wael Ghonim describes in the next chapter,
   today's social media is where the rules are being set
   for groups getting stuff done with no leaders. In
   many areas, **the role of a leader is becoming obsolete.** You need to be a power-user to understand and
   participate in these new norms as they evolve.

2. Get the hell offline!
   Follow the 80/20 rule:
   <20% of your connections will provide
   >80% of the power in your network.

Take the <20% to lunch.
Deepen your relationships with them.

Your Power Is in Your Network: Key Takeaways …

- Your network is the backbone of your life, work, career and goals.

- A lucky few may build fortunes or start revolutions simply due to the *size* of their network.
  But for most …

  The *depth* of your network — how deeply you are connected to each individual — will determine the depth and richness of your successes.

- You only get as good as you give.

For More: Click, The Journey Continues, page 202
  - How You Add Value Will Grow Your Tribe

HABIT 24
YOU ARE THE
POWERS THAT BE
INSIDERS NEVER TOPPLE THE STATUS QUO

"I believe in persistence, so I'm not an easy loser. I prefer to keep trying until I get what I want, or what I aspire to and what I believe should happen," says this hero.

"I have always been in competitive environments, feeling that I had to keep excelling — that I have to go beyond what I can currently do. I love the saying at Google, 'Great is not good enough.' You always have to keep fighting for what you believe in, even if you fail."

That's Wael Ghonim, an Internet activist, currently on sabbatical from his marketing role at Google. In 2011, he became an international figure and energized pro-democracy demonstrations in Egypt after his emotional interview following 11 days of secret incarceration by Egyptian police. His Facebook posting, "We are all Khaled Said," helped mobilize the Arab Spring revolution. Time magazine included Ghonim as one of the 100 most influential people of 2011.

Here's Ghonim on some of the lessons learned in toppling the status quo: "Right after Hosni Mubarak left, there was euphoria. Everybody felt the source of the problem is gone. Obviously, that was not the case. Because the problem was not in the people, it's in the system — the dynamics of how the country operates. What I came to learn is that it's going to be a journey, a tough one. We just have to make sure we're heading in the right direction. The situation in Egypt is not as much as we aspired to, and yet we are on a highway and we still have time to figure out how to get to the end. We need to celebrate the small successes and learn from our failures."

Insiders never overthrow the status quo because they have the most to lose if the system over which they preside collapses. That truth does not just apply to corrupt leaders or regimes overthrown in coups. That also applies to every upstanding corporate leader and every well-established product or service.

That is why we all must embrace …

In a disruptive world, you are the powers that be.

Don't wait for someone else to start your revolution.
Get off your ass and do it!

Ghonim reinforced this point when referring to where social media is taking us: "In a sense, the nature of social media makes the idea of having a leader who leads people obsolete.

Social media is more about empowering individuals and helping people believe in their aspirations. And in those networks you will find others who share those aspirations with you.

"I feel the most important thing in creating the changes we need," he continued, "is engagement and empowerment — making everyone part of the solution. The more frequently people use the Internet for health, education, fighting poverty, finding jobs, solving world problems, increasing tolerance among citizens of the world, the better everything will be."

He concluded by preparing all potential change-agents to complete the journey, whatever it takes: "Real change takes time. Be patient while being persistent."

Want Better Options?
Go Create Them!

We borrowed our chapter title from Umair Haque, who authored *The New Capitalist Manifesto: Building a Disruptively Better Business.*

Says Haque in a blog post about today's disruptive era, "The real problem is rebuilding the institutions that keep locking us into self-destructive choices. So how do the powers that be break out of that cage and resolve these dilemmas? They don't. In a radically decentralizing world, we are the powers that be. It's up to each of us to create better options."

It's up to you, and you, and you.

It's up to each of us.

Marcin Jakubowski believes this. He's on a quest to radically alter and disrupt many of the systems you use today.

Jakubowski is Founding Director of Open Source Ecology (OSE). He and OSE are building the Global Village Construction Set (GVCS): A set of the 50 most important machines that it takes to build a small civilization with modern comforts. Think of the GVCS as a Lego set for life-sized tools that are able to create entire infrastructures — ovens, wood splitters, cars, tractors and more.

"I have deep passion for constant growth," says Jakubowski. "I think innovation can increase by a factor of 100 if we were just more vulnerable and open to truly open collaboration on an economic front. Anybody who studies how things work will conclude that the current economic system is very inefficient. … I don't see any evidence that an inefficient system can be perpetuated forever. I believe the next economy is the open-source economy."

Jakubowski is not waiting for someone to take the lead on this revolution. He's making it happen according to his own vision:

"We're taking industry-standard tools and creating open-source, high-performance counterparts that cost less — for example, I'm building a 114-mile-per-gallon car, which I intend to be the last car I own."

No matter how big or small the disruption — rethinking an entire economy, or just how you make it through your day — if you want better options, it's up to you to create them.

C. Jimmy Lin figured that out as a little kid in his bathtub: "I remember thinking it should be more comfortable in there — so I invented little gadgets to make my bathtub experience better."

He's now focused on slightly more important issues: Lin is Founder of Rare Genomics Institute, a nonprofit biotech venture that micro-funds and enables genome sequencing for children with rare diseases.

He founded this firm and leverages crowd-funding to change the usual approach to medical research because, although an estimated 250 million people worldwide are suffering from rare diseases, few doctors or institutions are focused on cures. The economics of cures or better solutions just don't make sense — unless you're 39-year-old Gavin, who wakes up every day in pain; or 10-year-old Sabrina, who's gone through more testing than one can imagine; or the Chilean miner who brought his four year-old son, Jaoking, to the Mayo Clinic in the U.S. searching for answers and a diagnosis for his son, and left with none.

The status quo needs to change for those people and each and every one that Lin is fighting for.

"We just wanted to create an easier way to initiate research," says Lin. "Without the family needing to start a nonprofit, without them needing to pull together a scientific advisory board — we give them a quick solution in a box. Literally overnight we can start a project, get funding and bring researchers on board. Of course, the research takes time, but we get it started a lot faster than was previously possible. We want to empower and democratize scientific research.

"With any new idea," says Lin, "you have the people who love it, and then there's the old guard, who go, 'What are you doing? This is not how we do things. Having patients initiate science? This is kind of scary to us.'

"With ideas that change things, if you don't have anybody pushing back, that's a clue that you're not pushing hard enough."

Decision Time

You can play the game the way it's always been played, and pray that the next wave of disruption doesn't topple you.
… Or you can change the game and topple the status quo. One approach keeps you on the inside and not stepping on anyone's toes. The other will definitely put you in the line of fire — because if you're not pissing off somebody, then you're not really disrupting anything.

1. Pick something you are really, really passionate about.
   Something you believe is worth toppling the status quo for.

   That way, when the old guard gets pissed, you can laugh it off and keep going.

2. Reboot your brain.

   For many of us, the biggest challenge is not the old guard — it's that we carry over too much thinking from the old ways of doing things. Look at the examples in this chapter: Political revolution in the Mideast; rethinking capitalism; reinventing the historical approach to scientific research. These disruptions are taking off because their heroes were able to see the challenges in completely new ways.

You Are the Powers That Be: Key Takeaways ...

- Wait for no one to start your revolution. You are the powers that be.
- If you want something better, it's up to you to create it.
- If you're not pissing off somebody, you haven't gone far enough.

For More: Click, The Journey Continues, page 202
- You Can't Break Free If You Don't Know You're in a Cage

HABIT 25
IT'S NOT ABOUT YOU
WE ARE ALL DEPENDENT ON EACH OTHER

"I had no idea what I was getting into. I was asked to profile the first 12 children who were apprehended during the counterinsurgency. I was scared of them," she says after we promise to hide her face when sharing her interview.

"I soon realized that they were probably more scared of me, and that they were vulnerable, but not dangerous. But they had been made to behave in a very dangerous way — so they should be given an opportunity to change that."

That's Feriha Nazir Aziz Peracha, director and supervising psychologist for the Sabaoon Project, a school in the Swat valley of Pakistan. It was established to de-radicalize young boys after they had been indoctrinated into the Taliban. When they come to her, most no older than 12 or 13, they are filled with hatred, suspicion and defensiveness. Many have killed people, including their own townspeople, under the direction of the Taliban.

"I did nothing extraordinary," she says. "I just gave them good education, food, and psycho-social intervention for all the trauma they had been through and religious education, so they understood Islam and the Qur'an."

Yet she still lives with cautionary fear. Not only did she ask us to disguise her face, but she twice asked us to edit out certain portions of our interview to help ensure her safety.

So, how did she persevere? What did she call upon?

"As a child I went to a convent school, and I had to read scripture," she shares. "As I was raised Muslim, my mother was shocked: How could I learn scripture before I learned the Qur'an? My father said 'She's going to learn the Qur'an from the Bible. That's a book of God, too.'"

"That simple idea — that we are all connected — has influenced my entire life. It has made it easier. The divisions are gone. I don't know why in this day and age, where we communicate so fast, why these extreme views are prevailing still."

She concludes, "We are living in one global village. Us and them … you and me … at some point in time, we have to erase those lines, don't we?"

The most disruptive idea of all
is not about technology or change.
It's a timeless truth:
that we are all dependent on
each other.

Now is the time to erase the lines
between you and everyone else.

Andrew Zimmern learned this in the arid badlands of Botswana. Zimmern is a chef, host of *Bizarre Foods* and *Andrew Zimmern's Bizarre World*, author and teacher. He is teaching us all to eat our way to a better world.

"Defining ourselves by our differences seems to me to be absolutely ass backwards," Zimmern begins. "I thought that if I could show what people around the dinner table looked like, and show what they ate, drank, and talked about and fought about, that the people who watched my shows would think 'Wow, those folks in Madagascar are just like me and my family in my house in suburban Chicago.' Maybe then we could be a little more accepting of how other people spoke or dressed or about the color of their skin, or politics or spiritual beliefs. Eating together creates that bond. I've never had a meal with someone and gotten up and liked them less."

Zimmern continues by comparing his persona at home and abroad: "When I am at home, I lead a very safe existence. When I am on the road, I am a ballsy motherfucker. I will go into neighborhoods, ask questions — I never ask questions at home. There I know best, I know everything. When I'm on the road, I am not self-reliant, I become other-reliant. I become other-centered instead of self-centered.

"I was the least green person in the world until I went to Botswana and went hunting with a tribe there that uses snap snares to catch birds. They made some rope for us to catch these birds. It took us a couple days, but we caught a few. At one point, trying to be helpful, I took out my knife and went to cut the rope, and they freaked out! I'm like, 'What's the big deal? It's twine. I have balls of stuff like this in my garage.' They explained to me that they don't have individual possessions. It wasn't my rope to cut. It was the group's rope, and I shouldn't waste it. That Mother Earth gave them the plants to make the rope, and they had to kill a plant to get it. So you only take what you need."

Zimmern concludes, "I literally became a different person when I came home. We all have to be able to change and grow as human beings. Understanding our connection to others and what we can do for others is the best way to kickstart those behaviors."

Self-reliance can be a good thing.
It gets you some of what you need.

In a disruptive world, other-reliance
and being other-centered gets you
a lot more of what you need.
We are more united by what we
we have in common, and our
shared interdependence,
than we are divided by our differences.

Most every hero touched on this theme.

Tech investor Rusty Rueff says that the most crucial thing for society is for us to embrace inclusiveness and acceptance. Michael Murphy, an architect who is redesigning hospitals so they stop making us sicker, believes that stronger partnerships with all stakeholders is the only way to go. Cheryl Heller, who is Board Chair of PopTech and Program Chair of the School of Visual Arts Design for Social Innovation program, shared that major ahas come from knowing ourselves well enough to then let go and fully connect with others: "The wisdom is inside of us when we pay attention to it. When we look inside ourselves and we feel the connection to other people and to nature, we find we already know many of the answers to life's really important questions."

As we come to a close on the 25 successful habits for a disruptive world, we leave you in the mountains of India — with a story about our interconnectedness, which also relates back to Habit 23's theme of paying it forward.

"We were a bunch of kids hiking into the woods to a river," says Ajay Nityananda, a sustainability architect from India. "We reached the end of the path and had no idea where to go. An elderly man was there and came over to us, motioning for us to follow him. He said absolutely nothing to us, and wouldn't answer our questions. This goes on for *four hours*. Then he stops, points to the river, and just walks away. He wouldn't take anything from us in payment. He helped strangers and didn't want anything in return. This is why I do what I do now. My focus on sustainability and using the Earth's resources wisely is my way of repaying his kindness."

We are all dependent on our community and the kindness of strangers. We are all dependent on Mother Earth. We are all only as strong as the weakest among us.

Live your life accordingly.

It's Not About You: Key Takeaways ...

- The most disruptive idea of all is that we are all interconnected, we are all dependent on each other.
  Live your life accordingly.

For More: Click, The Journey Continues, page 202
- On Being a Sustainable Human Being

CODA
THE ONE
THING

> Curly: *You know what the secret to life is? …*
> *Just one thing. You stick to that and*
> *everything else don't mean shit.*
>
> Mitch: *That's great. But what's the one thing?*
>
> Curly: *That's what you gotta figure out.*
> — *City Slickers*

An encounter with Miki Agrawal is like experiencing pure energy. Her enthusiasm is nonstop, her joy radiates, and she clearly lives her life out loud.

Agrawal is Founder of both Slice and THINX, both based on solutions to her own personal needs.

With Slice, she is looking to save the world one all-natural and yummy slice of pizza at a time. She launched the pizza store because, with multiple nutritional issues, she was having trouble finding Manhattan eateries whose foods wouldn't upset her stomach. THINX is a women's underwear firm with the social mission to address the worldwide problem of ineffective and environmentally unsustainable women's products to manage their menstruation cycle. That too began with her own needs — menstruation challenges.

Speaking of THINX, she shares, "In my travels to Africa and India, I discovered that girls and women stay at home one week a month, and they use sticks, leaves, dirty rags, mud, bark … it's crazy. They end up dropping out of school or work because they get so far behind by losing one week a month — 100 million girls drop out every single year. It's staggering. And it's unfair, for something that's so natural — your period."

When speaking of lessons learned, Agrawal shared:

"Everything is figureoutable. It boils down to a pretty simple thing: Put one foot in front of the other and figure it out."

She concludes, "We all should be opening our eyes and seeing what sucks and taking the steps to fix that. People always assume that someone else is going to take care of it, but if everyone took personal initiative, then we'd have a much more exciting, vibrant world."

As far as how to survive and thrive and get stuff done in a disruptive world …

If you take away only one thing from this book, let it be this …

Everything is figureoutable.

No matter how disruptive things get:
Take one step at a time,
then figure it out as you go.

And here's something to remember while practicing that one thing. Cinda Boomershine shared, "I don't get my panties in a wad about anything, because I know we can work things out. I have a low tolerance for stupidity, but there are always solutions to challenges along the way."

Don't get your panties in a wad.
(Knickers, tighty whities, boxers … your choice.)

Have a sense of humor, dammit!
Don't take yourself, or anything,
too seriously.

Tribute
HONORING
NON-DISRUPTORS

Anchors. Voices of reason. Proven wisdom. We need that too.

Not everyone is called to be a disruptor.

Some of us are called to be anchors.

Disruptors are the change agents who rock our boats and won't allow us to settle for the status quo. Without them, the world would atrophy and eventually regress back into the Dark Ages.

But the world also needs balance. Too much disruption will take us the way of dinosaurs. Bang. Gone. Done.

That's why we also need people who will be the calming voice of reason. People who keep us grounded.

Sherlock needed Watson; Batman needed Alfred; Iron Man needed Pepper; Brain needed Pinky; King Lear needed the Fool; Luke needed Yoda.

The alter egos to each of these fictional characters represent a timeless concept. Adventurous disruptors always need someone who counterbalances them — wise, simple, solid and dependable people who have learned to weather the storms of life and bring that wisdom to the task at hand.

We all have a hero's journey to take if we are to find fulfillment. For some, that means shaking things up. For others, the journey is not as flashy — it is workmanlike: Getting things done, day in, day out. And that's oh-so-necessary to balance out the disruptor's journey.

Disruptors and the anchors of wisdom need each other. Not only that, they need to walk each other's paths from time to time. Disruptors need to learn to love and appreciate the ordinary, and the anchors need to be willing to step into disruptive shoes once in a while and shake things up.

Both paths must be honored, respected and shared.

You do not have to be the disruptor.

You can choose to be the anchor, the voice of reason.

But both roles must figure out how to benefit from, and take advantage of, and thrive in the midst of continuous disarray, disorder and disruption.

Thus, creating your own handbook from among the 25 habits.

Because, regardless of your role, the time in which you live is an age of continuous personal disruption.

CLICK
THE JOURNEY CONTINUES

Click is a free online toolkit that accompanies this book …

- What is a habit and how do you build one?
- How do you know when to *stop* questioning everything?
- How do you blow stuff up and get away with it?
- What are the first steps in becoming a triage master?
- How, *exactly*, does one have an affair on their boss?

… There were too may how-to tips to fit in this book.

So we created a How To Addendum.

Simply go to www.simplerwork.com/click to download this additional 54-page how-to toolkit.

We also included additional tips and advice from more of the 100 disruptive heroes. Our favorite comes from Salil Shetty, Secretary General for Amnesty International:

"Life's too short … not to be disruptive."

DISRUPTOR'S CHARACTER MAP

Mapping Character Traits to Successful Habits

When integrating both the character traits we found common among the 100 disruptive heroes (*The Courage Within Us*) and their habits/practices (*Disrupt!*), key patterns began to emerge.

The trait that drives the most best practices is **Trusting Your Gut and Values.** The ability to both survive all the disruptive chaos around you as well as leverage disruption for success depends mostly on you knowing yourself deeply, then acting accordingly.

After that comes **Insane Curiosity.** Those who survive and thrive during disruptive times are those who are passionate about constant learning/unlearning; they repeat that cycle forever.

The final character trait among the top three is the willingness to **Blow Stuff Up**. Those who do well in a disruptive world always carry with them a healthy dissatisfaction for the status quo.

See the table on the next pages to see more about how the traits and habits mapped to each other.

DISRUPTOR'S CHARACTER MAP

Comparing the findings from *The Courage Within Us* and *Disrupt!*

	Choose Your Parents Wisely	Beco Global
SUCCESSFUL HABITS		
Question Everything		
Audacity Matters		
Kill What You Cherish Most		
Do Epic Shit		
Blow Stuff Up		
Be a Triage Master		
Make a Mess		
Do It Anyway		
Go Faster		
Leap Before the Net Appears		
Simplify Constantly		
Have Lots of Affairs		
Go Back to the Future		
Fix the World's Flying Toilets		
Don't Fight Stupid		
Never Hesitate		
Never Accept Dingless Tools		
Don't Knock Down, Build Anew		
Know Thyself, Deeply	●	
Follow Your Passion	●	
Resilience Matters		
Disrupt Yourself		
Your Power Is in Your Network	●	
You Are the Powers That Be	●	
It's Not About You		

CHARACTER TRAITS

sanely ious	Blow Stuff Up	Trust Your Values, Trust Your Gut	Practice Failure As an Extreme Sport	Start With Lemonade Stands
●	●			
	●			
	●	●		
	●			
			●	
		●		
			●	
		●		
				●
●				
		●		
		●		
			●	
	●			
		●		
		●		
●				
	●			
		●		
		●		

DISRUPTOR'S PERSONAL DEVELOPMENT PLAN

1. MARK THE RESPONSES THAT BEST APPLY TO YOU

CHARACTER TRAITS	NEVER	SOME-TIMES	ALWAYS
Choose Your Parents Wisely How often do you select bosses, mentors and teammates because they will push you beyond your comfort zone and push you to increase your adventuring, exploring and risk-taking?	◯	◯	◯
Become a Global Citizen How often do you seek to learn about the needs, desires and inequalities experienced by individuals and cultures that are completely different from you or unfamiliar to you?	◯	◯	◯
Be Insanely Curious How often do you get feedback or comments that you are an insatiable learner and/or that you will not rest until you find better ways to do things?	◯	◯	◯
Blow Stuff Up How often do you work on *radically* changing inefficiencies (where your focus is on liberating an individual's time and energy, not just on cost-saving inefficiencies), or imbalances, or hardships on others in order to make things a lot better for more people? (Incremental improvements don't count here.)	◯	◯	◯
Trust Your Values, Trust Your Gut How often do you trust your gut when taking action, regardless of what your boss or the plan says you're "supposed" to do?	◯	◯	◯
Practice Failure As an Extreme Sport How often do you seek to increase your failure rate — for the sole purpose of making your final effort better?	◯	◯	◯
Start With Lemonade Stands How often are you the sole or primary person responsible for bottom-line profits and losses?	◯	◯	◯

2. SCORE YOUR RESULTS

Four or more NEVERs: Disruption Newbie

Seek personal one-on-one coaching in some of the 25 disruptive habits. (First, see Character Map [page 204] for which habits are linked to which character traits. Then see the download below for exercises and how-to's relating to those habits.)

Four or more SOMETIMEs: Some experience as a Disruptive Hero, with lots of room for improvements

Self-instruction: Select from and the use tools below.

Four or more ALWAYS: Disruptive Master.

You should have written this book! Quit your day job. Travel the countryside in a robe, with a staff, teaching others how to master disruption. (Or keep your day job, but still teach others.)

3. DOWNLOAD THE FREE TOOL THAT ACCOMPANIES DISRUPT!

Disrupt! includes a bonus how-to download for each of the 25 disruptive habits, which is available to you too. Use the 25 habits to work up your personal development plan.

For example, if you scored *Never* or *Sometimes* on the character trait Blow Stuff Up — then after you download this free tool, focus on the habits associated with that trait (found on page 205): Audacity Matters, Kill What You Cherish Most, Do Epic Shit, BlowStuff Up, Never Accept Dingless Tools, Disrupt Yourself. That's the beginning of the work you'll need to do.

DOWNLOAD...

To download this free tool, go to www.simplerwork.com/click.

I would never attempt to cross-sell you (ahem) ...

But if you're looking for lots of in-depth details on the 7 essential character traits, then please do check out *The Courage Within Us*. Lots there to build out a disruptive development plan.

ACKNOWLEDGMENTS

Thank You!

Making sense out of continuous disruptions: These are the people who kept me grounded as I pursued that lofty goal ...

Family. Disruptions happen, even in families. As did with mine. Thank you Ian and Desi, Taylor and Stephen for keeping me somewhat sane and very loved throughout this project. Couldn't have done this without you!

Work-in-Progress Counselors and Readers. Someone had to tell me when I was full of myself and when my babblings were incoherent. Among a cast of hundreds, these folks deserve special mention for performing that service: Nikita Arora, Papitha Cader, John Caswell, Kim Ann Curtin, Johan D'Haeseleer, Bob Franco, Joe Fratoni, Steve Gardiner, John Gerstner, Dave Gray, Stacy Marie Ishmael, David Jardin, Bev Kaye, Mark Koskiniemi, Jody Lentz, Mark Leyba, Eileen McDargh, Tanveer Naseer, Lionel Nicolas, David Physick, Whitney Quesenbery, Theresa Quintanilla, Robert Rapplean, Toby Sinats, Sharrann Simmons, Camille Smith, Patti Warkentin, Graham Westwood, Mike Wittenstein, Jason Womack. Thanks guys!

Searchmeisters. We scoured the world for disruptors. Three people deserve extra thanks for their help in finding so many great heroes: Sunny Bates, Michael Giuliano and Josh Klein.

Book Teammates. Nothing you read would have been possible without the Herculean efforts and sweat equity investments of the Net Minds team, headed by Tim Sanders, as well as my tireless and amazing editor Michael Martin. Thank you two so much! And then there are the wonderful teammates who handled everything from transcribing and mapping the interviews, to copyediting, to design and production, to publicity and more. My huge thanks go to Dan Boudwin, Jenny Burman, Mark Novelli/Imago, Pilar Wyman and Cave Henricks Communications.

100+ Heroes. I didn't really author this book, they did. My huge thanks to all of the heroes who gave so much, so generously!

You. This book is nothing without your ahas and actually putting it to use. Thank you for adding that missing ingredient!

INDEX

100+ GREAT DISRUPTIVE HEROES

Countries Represented

Disruptors are everywhere. Here's where we found our heroes: Afghanistan, Argentina, Australia, Belgium, Canada, Chile, China, Egypt, Finland, France, Germany, Great Britain, India, Ireland, Italy, Japan, Kenya, Kuwait, Mexico, Netherlands, Pakistan, Singapore, Scotland, Spain, Turkey, United Arab Emirates, Uganda, United States, Venezuela

About the List

Among our 100 Great Heroes are some of the super-elite people creating disruptive changes. But finding only 100 super-elite heroes was not our goal. We also specifically sought unsung heroes, failed-and-struggling-back heroes, ordinary people who achieved something extraordinary, and people from all walks of life. In other words, whoever you are, we wanted you to see yourself among the 100.

We built the list mainly through referrals. We began with about a dozen heroes, then asked everyone we interviewed: "Whom do you admire? Who's your hero? Who's doing amazing disruptive work?" That produced more than 1,000 names, from which Bill Jensen and a panel of experts selected the best cross section.

And just when we thought we had it down to 100, more possible interviews would pop up. So, like a baker's dozen, we kind of cheated — the list is now titled 100+ Great Disruptive Heroes.

About the Videos

Before you watch: Consider your expectations managed! HD, not. Video quality depended on Internet connection speeds — most are good to fair. Some are, uh, let's generously say less than good. However, all content is awesome! **Searching:** The e-version of this book contains links to every video. If you are reading the print-version, go to YouTube and search "Disruptive Heroes (Person's Name)."

About the Quotes

If you search for them, you will find minor differences between what you see in the interviewees' videos and what's in print. That is because a) full interviews were longer than what's in video highlights, so some quotes are available only in print; and b) people speak differently than they would write, and some asked for cleanups; and c) with interviewee participation, print-quotes were edited for clarity, space and segues between ideas. Each interviewee reviewed the final edited print-quotes.

About Both Books

We asked two particular questions of all heroes: "What makes you ... you?" and "What lessons have you learned about disruption?" That approach ultimately led us to two separate books: *The Courage Within Us* is a short e-book about the character traits needed for an era of disruption. *Disrupt!* covers what we need to do and how we need to do it. By using the same heroes' interviews for both, some overlaps did occur. We worked hard to ensure that no more than 5 percent of exact quotes or content appeared in both books.

100+ GREAT DISRUPTIVE HEROES

NORA ABOUSTEIT, Founder, Kollabora

MIKI AGRAWAL, Founder, Slice and THINX

RADHA AGRAWAL, Founder, Super Sprowtz

MUMTAZ ALI, Founder, UM Healthcare

DAVID AUERBACH, LINDSAY STRADLEY, Founders, Sanergy

CHRIS BALME, Founder, Spark

KEN BANKS, Founder, kiwanja.net

SUNNY BATES, World-Changing Networker, Connector

DEBBIE BEREBICHEZ, The Science Babe, Science Educator

BEN BERKOWITZ, Founder, SeeClickFix.com

MANICK BHAN, Founder, Rukkus

JAN BOELEN, Artistic Director, Z33

CINDA BOOMERSHINE, Owner, cinda b USA

BRIAN BORDAINICK, Founder, 9th Ward Field of Dreams

ADAM BORELLI, Former Executive Director, New Leaders Council

SASKIA BRUYSTEN, Co-Founder, Yunus Social Business

GIB BULLOCH, Executive Director, Accenture Development Partnerships

GARRETT CAMP, Founder, StumbleUpon

PARIK CHOPRA, Senior Director, Brand Strategy, Philips Lighting

JERRY COMYN, ex-Ad Man, "Shove it" Resignation Went Viral

JOHN DANNER, Founder, Rocketship Education

TIBURCIO DE LA CÁRCOVA, Founder, Santiago Makerspace

ELISABET DE LOS PINOS, Founder, Aura Biosciences

MARCO DE ROSSI, Founder, Oil Project

AARON DIGNAN, Founder, Undercurrent

ANNIE DUKE, Professional Poker Player

ULLA ENGESTRÖM, Founder, ThingLink

CATERINA FAKE, Founder, Flickr, Hunch

DAVID FLINK, Founder, Eye to Eye

MAT FOGARTY, Founder, Crowdcast

GREG GAGE, Co-Founder, Backyard Brains

LARA GALINSKY, SVP, Echoing Green

CINDY GALLOP, Founder, MakeLoveNotPorn.com

RIKIN GANDHI, Founder, Digital Green

LISA GANSKY, Founder, Ofoto

WAEL GHONIM, Online Revolutionary, Arab Spring Revolution

BOB GIRALDI, Original *Mad Man*, Film, Commercials

JOHN GERACI, Founder, DIY City

JUDE GOERGEN, DAVID PURPERA, Creative Team Members, SBN Interactive

MARK GOLDRING, CEO, Oxfam Great Britain

MATÍAS GUTIÉRREZ, Director, R&D, Bioquimica.cl

JOHN HAGEL, Co-Chair, Deloitte Center for the Edge

TONY HAILE, GM, Chartbeat

TYLER HARTUNG, Founder, Unreasonable Institute

DICKIE HASKELL, Trustafarian, Living off the Grid

SCOTT HEIFERMAN, Founder, Meetup

JEREMY HEIMANS, Founder, Purpose

BETTINA HEIN, Founder, Pixability

CHERYL HELLER, Chair, SVA Social Innovation MFA Program

BETHANY HENDERSON, Founder, City Hall Fellows

JAMIE HEYWOOD, Founder, PatientsLikeMe

MADISON HILDEBRAND, Realtor, Media Personality

BOB HINTY, Owner, Hentz Manufacturing

ANDREW HORN, Founder, Ability List

SARA HOROWITZ, Founder, Freelancers Union

YAO HUANG, Founder, The Hatchery

MARCIN JAKUBOWSKI, Founder, Open Source Ecology

LEAH BERGER JENSEN, (no relation to the author), Tulane School of Medicine

CENK KARASAPAN, Entrepreneur

MICHAEL KARNJANAPRAKORN, Founder, Skillshare

GUY KAWASAKI, Former chief evangelist of Apple; Co-Founder, Alltop.com

CHERYL KISER, Executive Director, Babson Social Innovation Lab

ERIC KNAUF, Senior Manager, Talent Management, Ariba

JOSH KNOWLES, Social Media/Gaming Designer

VISHEN LAKHIANI, Founder, Mindvalley

GERT LANCKRIET, Associate Professor, UC San Diego

JON LANDAU, Producer, *Avatar, Titanic*

FRANCOISE LEGOUES, VP, Innovation, CIO's Office, IBM

C. JIMMY LIN, Founder, Rare Genomics Institute

CV MADHUKAR, Founder, PRS Legislative Research

MARISSA MAYER, CEO, Yahoo

ANDREW McAFEE, Web 2.0/3.0 Researcher, MIT Sloan School

JULIE McCARTHY, NPR Correspondent, Peabody Award Winner

TARYN MILLER-STEVENS, Founder, MBM, Executive Retreats

UMEED MISTRY, Dive Instructor

SANGA MOSES, Founder, Eco-Fuel Africa

DOMINIC MUREN, Founder, The Humblefactory

MICHAEL MURPHY, Founder, MASS Design Group

MEGAN MURRAY, Collaborative Strategist, Moxie Software

CHRIS NAEGELIN, Co-Founder, Spotflux

DEEPA NARAYAN, Poverty and Development Advisor

ANDY NEWTON, Director, SE Coast Ambulance Service

KENNETH NG, CEO, Asia Pacific, American Standard

AJAY NITYANANDA, Sustainability Architect

PRIYA PARKER, Conflict Mediator, Innovation Labs

FERIHA PERACHA, Director, Sabaoon Project

SEAN PETERS, Founder, Global Catalyst Initiative

DAN PONTEFRACT, Senior Director, Learning, Telus

JAKE PORWAY, Founder, DataKind

NITIN RAO, Founder, Sunglass

AISHWARYA RATAN, Director, Microsavings/Payment Initiative

CAMILLE REBELO, Founder, EcoPlanet Bamboo

JESSE ROBBINS, Founder, Opscode

ALEC ROSS, Innovation Advisor

TIM ROWE, Founder, Cambridge Innovation Center

RUSTY RUEFF, Former CEO, SNOCAP, Tech Investor

JESSICA SAGER, JANNA WAGNER, Founders, All Our Kin

BERT SANDIE, Director or Technical Excellence, Electronic Arts

SALIL SHETTY, Secretary General, Amnesty International

DAVID SINCLAIR, Creator, Sinclair Method: Cure for Alcoholism

KARLA TANKERSLEY, Supply Chain Engineer

DON TAPSCOTT, Chairman, Moxie Insight

TONY TENICELA, Global Leader, Workforce Diversity/LGBT Markets, IBM

SAKU TUOMINEN, Founder, Idealist Group

GENTRY UNDERWOOD, Founder, Orchestra, Inc.

STEFAAN VAN HOOYDONK, Philips Lighting University

MARTÍN VARSAVSKY, Founder, Fon

MARIQUEL WAINGARTEN, Founder, Hickies

JIMMY WALES, Founder, Wikipedia

SCOTT WARREN, Founder, Generation Citizen

HENRIK WERDELIN, Managing Partner, Prehype

ANDREW ZIMMERN, Chef, Host, *Bizarre Foods*

ABOUT THE AUTHOR

Mr. Simplicity

Bill Jensen makes it easier to do great work.

Bill is today's foremost expert on work complexity and cutting through clutter to what really matters.

He has spent the past two decades studying how work gets don (Much of what he's found horrifies him.)

He is an internationally-acclaimed author and speaker who is known for provocative ideas, extremely useful content, and his passion for making it easier for everyone to work smarter, not harder.

His books:

- *Simplicity*
- *Work 2.0*
- *Simplicity Survival Handbook*
- *What Is Your Life's Work?*
- *Hacking Work*
- *The Courage Within Us*
- *Disrupt!*

He is CEO of The Jensen Group, a change consulting firm he founded in 1985. He lives in Morristown, New Jersey, travels the world for clients and sneaks in fun-time wherever he goes.

Most valuable valueless possession: 1950's cardboard box tha resided in a hall closet in his childhood home. On the side, in Mom's handwriting: *Bill's Mittens, Hats, Scarves*

Personal life fantasy: To bicycle around the globe via brewerie

bill@simplerwork.com
www.simplerwork.com
@simpletonbill